TRANSLATIONS OF EASTERN POETRY AND PROSE

PLATE I

A BATTLE-SCENE IN THE *SHÁHNÁMA*

TRANSLATIONS OF EASTERN POETRY AND PROSE

BY

REYNOLD A. NICHOLSON
LITT.D., LL.D.
LECTURER IN PERSIAN IN THE UNIVERSITY OF CAMBRIDGE
FORMERLY FELLOW OF TRINITY COLLEGE

CAMBRIDGE
AT THE UNIVERSITY PRESS
1922

CAMBRIDGE
UNIVERSITY PRESS

University Printing House, Cambridge CB2 8BS, United Kingdom

Published in the United States of America by Cambridge University Press, New York

Cambridge University Press is part of the University of Cambridge.

It furthers the University's mission by disseminating knowledge in the pursuit of education, learning and research at the highest international levels of excellence.

www.cambridge.org
Information on this title: www.cambridge.org/9781107631922

First published 1922
First paperback edition 2013

A catalogue record for this publication is available from the British Library

ISBN 978-1-107-63192-2 Paperback

IN MEMORIAM

CAROLI JACOBI LYALL

POESEOS ARABICAE ANTIQUAE

EDITORIS DOCTISSIMI

INTERPRETIS ET INGENIO ET ARTE

PRAESTANTISSIMI

PREFACE

THIS book, containing versions from about fifty authors, may be of use to some who are interested in the two great literatures of Islam—Arabic and Persian. Theology, law, philosophy, science and medicine are scarcely touched, but the reader will learn something of Islamic history and religion, morals and manners, culture and character; something, too, of the heathen Arabs to whom Mohammed was sent. I have not, however, selected with a view to instruction. All the poetry, and the chief part of the prose, has been chosen for its merit as literature; and my choice was guided by the belief that translators do best in translating what they have enjoyed. If the present collection appeals in the first place to lovers of poetry and *belles-lettres*, it has gained in solidity and range of interest by including passages from famous biographers and historians like Ibn Hishám, Mas'údí, Ṭabarí, and Ibn Khaldún. The extracts, which are mostly short and seldom run beyond the five pages allowed by such a good judge as Mr A. R. Waller, cover a period of a thousand years from the beginning of the 6th to the end of the 15th century A.D. The arrangement is chronological, and in order to preserve the connexion of Persian with Arabian literary history Persian writers (distinguished by asterisks) keep their place in the series instead of being grouped apart.

As a rule, the poetry has been turned into verse, which can give the artistic effect better than prose, though it cannot render the meaning so exactly[1]. Yet the power of verse to

[1] Generally the verse-translations are faithful without being literal, but in one piece from Imra'u 'l-Ḳais and in a few from Ḥáfiẓ I have taken the same kind of liberty which FitzGerald used in his version of Omar Khayyám.

fulfil its aim is limited by circumstances. While any poem can be reproduced in metre, few Arabic or Persian poems are wholly suitable for English verse: we must decide what to translate, and especially what *not* to translate, before considering how it shall be done. I disagree with the opinion that success may turn on the existence in the translator's language of a native form and manner corresponding; but undoubtedly advantage should be taken of such models when possible. For example, it seems to me that parts of the *Sháhnáma* have much in common with Scott's metrical romances, and that a version which recognises this affinity and avails itself of these associations is more likely to please the English reader than one which ignores them. Rhyme is an indispensable element in Arabic and Persian poetry, and there are other reasons why it should not be abandoned willingly by translators who use English metres. For one thing, unrhymed couplets soon become tedious, while in unconfined blank verse every trace of the original form disappears. Now and then I have copied the monorhyme of Oriental odes, but it is not easy to do so in poems of any length, nor is it worth the trouble. Far more depends on the choice of a metre consorting with the tone, spirit, and movement of the original. The scholarly version of the *Sháhnáma* by A. G. and E. Warner fails, I think, here. Admitting that the task of the translators was heavy enough to justify their refusal of rhyme, every one acquainted with the Persian must feel the difference between their sedate and slow-marching verse and the lively, rapid, and resonant metre in which Firdausí wrote[1].

[1] Professor Browne has published several very good specimens of translation in alliterative verse (*Literary History of Persia*, vol. I, pp. 140–150). I cannot help thinking, however, that this somewhat rude and archaic style is incapable of doing justice to the dignity and refinement of Firdausí's poem.

Sir Charles Lyall, who, about a year before his death, honoured me by accepting the dedication of this book in token of my admiration for his renderings of the old Arabian poetry, has imitated the Arabic metres with peculiar skill; and some of my versions adopt the same method. These metres are quantitative while their equivalents in a European language must be accentual, so that the English measure can only suggest the Oriental rhythm. Perhaps the specimens given below will serve to indicate how the two are related to each other. As regards the method itself, experiment has convinced me that in Arabic, at any rate, a verse-translation is more apt to convey the right impression when the original form is partially reproduced in this way. Besides, as Sir Charles Lyall pointed out, the accentual types of the *Ṭawíl* and *Kámil* metres now belong to English poetry, Browning having employed them both, sometimes regularly but oftener with variations, in *Abt Vogler* and *Muléykeh.*

In selecting the five illustrations reproduced by Mr R. B. Fleming from manuscripts in the British Museum, I sought the help and advice of my friend Mr Edward Edwards, and I think it will be acknowledged that I have every reason to be grateful to him. The frontispiece (*Add.* 27,257, f. 445 *a*) depicts a battle between two Indian princes, Gau and Ṭalḥand (*Sháhnáma*, ed. Macan, IV, 1737 foll.), but suits almost as well the poem on p. 97 where 'Unṣurí describes a campaign of Sultan Maḥmúd of Ghazna, in which also elephants took part. Those numbered II, III and IV illustrate the same passages as the original miniatures (*Add.* 18,188, f. 183 *a*; *Or.* 1200, f. 29 *b* and f. 34 *a*). The first shows Rustam letting down a lasso to Bízhan in order to draw him out of his dungeon; on the left of Rustam stands Manízha, the heroine of Firdausí's tale. In III and IV we see an immortal character in Arabian fiction, Abú Zaid of Sarúj, whose adventures were written by Ḥarírí. The fifth illustration (*Or.* 4566, f. 6) is a portrait of the Persian mystic and poet, Farídu'ddín 'Aṭṭár. This has a remarkable individuality, and though it cannot be contemporary with 'Aṭṭár I should like to believe that there is some genuine tradition behind it.

I. The *Ṭawíl* (Long) Metre.

⏑ − − | ⏑ − − | − | ⏑ − ⏑ | ⏑ − − − ‖
aḳimu | bani ummi | ṣudura | maṭiyikum ‖

⏑ − − | ⏑ − − − | ⏑ − − | ⏑ − ⏑ −
fa'inni | 'ila ḳaumin | siwakum | la'amyalu.

Aríse, O | my móther's sóns, | and bréast with | your stéeds the níght,

For trúly | the lóve I béar | is kínder | to sóme less kín.

⏑ − − | ⏑ − − − | ⏑ − ⏑ | ⏑ − − ⏑ − ‖
tasamma | sururan ja | hilun mu | takharriṣun ‖

⏑ ⏑ − | ⏑ − − − | ⏑ − − ⏑ | ⏑ − − −
bi-fihi 'l- | bara hal fi 'l- | zamani | sururu.

He gáve to | hímself the náme | of Jóy—fóol | and líar hé!

May éarth stop | his móuth! In Tíme | is ány | thing jóyful?

II. The *Kámil* (Perfect) Metre.

⏑ − ⏑ − ⏑ − | ⏑⏑ − − ⏑ − | ⏑ − ⏑ − − ‖
fa-waḳaftu 'as | 'aluha wa-kai | fa su'aluna ‖

− − − ⏑ − | ⏑⏑ − − ⏑ − | ⏑ − ⏑ − ⏑ −
ṣumman khawa | lida ma yabi | nu kalamuha.

And I stópped to ásk | whither góne are théy?— | what aváils to ásk

Things hárd of héar | ing and dárk of spéech | that abíde unchánged?

III. The *Wáfir* (Ample) Metre.

⏑ − − − | ⏑ − ⏑ ⏑ − | ⏑ − − ‖
fa-ma far'u 'l- | fatati 'idha | tawarat ‖

⏑ − − ⏑ − | ⏑ − − − | ⏑ − ⏑
bi-muftaḳirin | 'ila sarḥin | wa-ḍafri.

No néed, when in éarth | the máid résts cóv | ered óver,

No néed for her lócks | of háir to be lóosed | and pláited.

IV. The *Basíṭ* (Wide) Metre.

ma 'l-khairu ṣau | mun yadhu | bu 'l-ṣa'imu | na lahu ||

wa-la ṣala | tun wa-la | ṣufun 'ala 'l- | jasadi.

Vírtue is neí | ther a fást | consúming thóse | who it kéep,

Nor ány óff | ice of práyer | nor róugh fleece wrápped | on the límbs.

V. The *Madíd* (Tall) Metre.

ḥallati 'l-kham | ru wa-ka | nat ḥaraman ||

wa-bi-la'yin | ma 'alam | mat taḥillu.

Láwful nów to | mé is wíne, | lóng forbídden:

Sóre the strúggle | ére the bán | was o'errídden.

This rare measure is represented by a single example (No. 16), which does not correspond very closely with the original.

Many of the verse-translations have appeared before, and I wish to thank Messrs. G. Bell and Sons, J. M. Dent and Sons, T. Fisher Unwin, and the Syndics of the Cambridge University Press for permission to reprint them. Nearly all the prose versions are new; of those in verse twenty-five are now published for the first time: Nos. 7, 11–15, 19, 20, 25–29, 31, 34, 37, 38, 55, 63, 143–148. In an appendix I have supplied references to the Arabic and Persian texts from which the versions were made. Though specialists will find in this anthology much that is well-known to them, it includes comparatively few pieces that were already translated into English by other hands.

REYNOLD A. NICHOLSON.

December, 1921.

ALPHABETICAL LIST OF AUTHORS

LIST OF ILLUSTRATIONS

TRANSLATIONS
OF EASTERN POETRY AND PROSE

Murra of Shaibán

Some of the oldest Arabic poems that have come down to us are connected with the War of Basús, which broke out in the early years of the sixth century A.D. between the brother-tribes of Bakr and Taghlib. Murra belonged to Shaibán, a subdivision of Bakr. He had a son, Jassás, and a daughter, Ḥalíla, who was married to Kulaib, the chief of Taghlib. Jassás quarrelled with Kulaib and murdered him. At first, Murra was for surrendering his guilty son, but when the elders of Shaibán resolved to fight rather than give him up, Murra turned to him and said:

I

If war thou hast wrought and brought on me,
No laggard I with arms outworn.
Whate'er betide, I make to flow
The baneful cups of death at morn.

When spear-heads clash, my wounded man
Is forced to drag the spear he stained.
Never I reck, if war must be,
What Destiny hath preordained.

Donning war's harness, I will strive
To fend from me the shame that sears.
Already I thrill and my lust is roused
For the shock of the horsemen against the spears!

Al-Find

When war began, the other clans of Bakr held aloof, deeming Shaibán in the wrong, until an event happened which caused them to rise as one man. Bujair, the nephew of Ḥárith ibn 'Ubád, was treacherously slain by Muhalhil, Kulaib's brother, notwithstanding that Ḥárith and his family had hitherto taken no part in the struggle. On hearing this, Ḥárith declared that if vengeance were satisfied by the death of Bujair, he would be content, but

Muhalhil replied, "I have only taken satisfaction for Kulaib's shoe-latchet." Then Ḥárith sprang up in wrath, crying:

"God knows, I kindled not this fire, although
I am burned in it to-day.
A lord for a shoe's latchet is too dear:
To horse! To horse! Away!"

And al-Find said on the same occasion:

2

We spared the Banú Hind[1] and said, "Our brothers they remain:
It may be Time will make of us one people yet again."
But when the wrong grew manifest, and naked Ill stood plain,
And naught was left but violence, we paid them bane for bane.
As lions marched we forth to war in rage and fierce disdain,
Our swords brought widowhood and tears and wailing in their train,
Our spears dealt gashes wide whence blood like water spilled amain.
No way but force to weaken force and mastery obtain;
'Tis wooing contumely to meet wild actions with humane:
By evil thou mayst win to peace when good is tried in vain.

Jaḥdar son of Ḍubai'a

At last the Bakrites prepared for a decisive battle, shaved their heads, and vowed to conquer or die. Jaḥdar son of Ḍubai'a was an ill-favoured dwarfish man with fair flowing love-locks, and he said, "O my people, if ye shave my head, ye will disfigure me. Leave my locks for the first horseman of Taghlib that shall ride forth from the glen to-morrow (I will answer for him)"; and he chanted these verses:

3

To wife and daughter
Henceforth I am dead:
Dust for ointment
On my hair is shed.

[1] Hind was the mother of Bakr and Taghlib, after whom the two tribes descended from them are named. Here "Banú Hind" (the sons of Hind) refers to the Taghlibites.

Let me close with the horsemen
Who hither ride!
Shear my locks from me
If I stand aside!

Well wots a mother
If the son she bore
And swaddled on her bosom
And smelt him o'er,

Whenever warriors
In the mellay meet,
Is a puny weakling
Or a man complete!

Muhalhil son of Rabí'a

He was the brother of Kulaib and succeeded him as chief of Taghlib.

4

O night we are passing at Dhú Ḥusum, shine forth into dawn when thou art ended, and return not!
If my night at al-Dhaná'ib hath been long[1], yet was I used to weep for the shortness of the night.
Meseems the Kid, the Kid of the Wain, sinks prone on his forelegs in a rolling sky,
Whilst Sirius and his twin star creep towards Canopus, which gleams like the crown of an aged camel.
Were the graveyards dug up, so that Kulaib might be uncovered and know at al-Dhaná'ib what a "visitor of women[2]"
I proved myself on the day of al-Shu'batán, his eye would be gladdened—but how shall we meet them that are under the tombs?
And lo, at Wáridát I have left Bujair in a flow of blood like the unguent mixed with saffron:

[1] Because it was "a night of memories and of sighs." The grave of Kulaib was at al-Dhaná'ib in the north-eastern borders of Najd (*Aghání*, IV, 142).
[2] Kulaib is said to have applied these words to his brother, of whose warlike prowess he had no high opinion.

By slaying him I tore the tents of the Banú 'Ubád—and some deed of violence is most healing to stricken hearts—
Albeit he doth not pay fully for Kulaib, such a man as my brother was when the women rush forth from their bowers[1].
And Hammám son of Murra: him too we have left low, over him the huge male vulture,
Heaving up his breast in which the spear is fixed, while another great brute like a camel is tugging at him.
And were it not for the wind, those in Ḥajr would be made to hear the clang of helmets smitten by our swordblades.
My life for the Banú Shaḳíḳa[2]! the day they came like lions of the jungle that persevered in roaring,
As though their spears were the ropes of a deep well whose walls are wide apart[3],
On the morn when beside 'Unaiza we and the sons of our father[4] were (grinding one another) as two mill-stones turned by hand,
And our horses standing over them all day, the horses (sweating) as though washed in a water-pool[5].

Imra'u 'l-Ḳais

Author of the most famous of the *Mu'allaḳát*. He was a grandson of King Ḥárith of Kinda. His father, Ḥujr, ruled for some time over the Banú Asad in central Arabia, and when they revolted and put him to death, Imra'u 'l-Ḳais came forward to avenge him. After many adventures, he set out for Constantinople, where he was honourably received by the Emperor Justinian. He died on his way back, about A.D. 540. The cause of his death is said to have been a poisoned robe sent to him by Justinian, with whose daughter he had an intrigue. Imra'u 'l-Ḳais is the oldest of the great Arabian poets and the mightiest in genius. His daring images and exquisitely worded pictures of life in the desert set

[1] On the approach of the enemy. [2] The Taghlibites.
[3] *I.e.* their spears were long and straight (like the rope or cord by which a bucket is let down into a well) and numerous (because in a wide well there is room for many ropes). Another point of comparison is that spears draw blood as ropes draw water.
[4] The Bakrites. See p. 2, note 1.
[5] *I.e.* "We pursued them hotly and stripped the dead at our leisure."

the translator a hard task, which the state of the text only makes harder. The first specimen given here belongs to the *Mu'allaḳa*; the second is a very free, and the third a more literal rendering of passages in two of the minor odes.

5

How many a noble tent hath oped its treasure
To me, and I have ta'en my fill of pleasure,
Passing the warders who with eager speed
Had slain me, if they might but hush the deed,
What time in heaven the Pleiades unfold
A belt of orient gems distinct with gold!
I entered. By the curtain there stood she,
Clad lightly as for sleep, and looked on me.
"By God," she cried, "what recks thee of the cost?
I see thine ancient madness is not lost."
I led her forth, she trailing as we go
Her broidered skirt lest any footprint show,
Until beyond the tents the valley sank
With curving dunes and many a pilèd bank.
Toward me I drew her then by side-locks both,
Nor she—full-ankled, fine of waist—was loth.
Fair in her colour, splendid in her grace,
Her bosom smooth as mirror's polished face:
A white pale virgin pearl such lustre keeps,
Fed with clear water in untrodden deeps.
Half-turned away, a slant soft cheek, and eye
Of timid antelope with fawn close by,
She lets appear; and lo, the shapely neck
Not bare of ornament, else without a fleck,
Whilst from her shoulders in profusion fair,
Like clusters on the palm, down falls her coal-dark hair.

6

Love that wellnigh had ceased from welling,
Love rose high in my heart again
For Sulaimà, down in 'Arar dwelling,
When Taimar's rills were alive with rain.

Oh, I see thee, Kinána's daughter,
And the howdahs in the mist of dawn
Gliding by, like ships on water—
They passed and thou wert gone!—
Like tall palms undeflowered,
For the sword of their clan is drawn
Until their maiden
Boughs be laden
With ripe yellow bunches and lowered,
A wonder to look upon!
Proudly the sons of Rabdá ride
At harvest-tide.

But the women those howdahs nestled,
More fair seemed they
Than statues, on marble chiselled,
Of Suḳf, in the valley where Sájúm
Foams to the Persian bay.
Safely fended,
Softly tended,
With pearls and rubies and beads of gold
And gums of delicate odour in pyxes old,
Spicy musk and aloes and myrrh—
Sweet, oh, sweet is the breath of her
Who stole from thee, Sulaimà, my love away.

The cord is cut asunder that tied me so true of yore,
When darting a covert eye to thy tent close-veiled
I saw thee and paled
And trembled at the sight,
As one trembles who overnight
Drank deep, and in the morning his cup is filled once more.

7

(Metre: *Ṭawíl.*)

And oft in the early morn, when birds in their nests are still,
I ride whither he that comes to forage must fare alone—
A spring-pasture, one kept safe by spear-heads in watch and ward,

And rich with the floods poured forth from many a black
storm-cloud—
On stout mare, a bay whose flesh her running made dry and
tough,
As though 'twere, so hard is it, the staff of a weaver's beam.
I scared once with her a herd of wild-kine: their skins pure
white,
Unblemished; their legs bestriped like needle-wrought
Yemen robes.
Meseemed, as they sped their pace and trotted, I saw a troop
Of horses that wheel about, with glistening saddle-cloths.
So wheeled they and set on guard behind them a lusty bull
Of long back and horn: his nose turns upward, his tail
sweeps low;
Whilst I in pursuit bore on against bull and cow alike,
And bent to the chase, what time I followed it, all my mind.
As swift as an eagle swoops and softly her wings draws in
To snatch in the morning-shine a hare on Sherabba's height—
Her eyrie around lie fresh and shrivelled the hearts of birds,
As though the jujube's red fruit were mingled with crumbling
dates—
The foxes that haunt Arwál have slunk to their holes in fear:
So under me flew the steed I hastened with hand and thighs.

Were that after which I strive my bare need, to live withal,
For me were a little wealth enough: I would seek no more;
But after renown I strive, a firm glory rooted deep,
And men such as I may win the glory most deep and firm.
How long in a man soe'er the breath of his spirit lasts,
He never will reach the end of craving or cease from toil.

Ṭarafa

He took part, it is said, in the War of Basús and afterwards visited the court of Ḥíra (near ancient Babylon), the capital of the Lakhmite kingdom. He had a bitter tongue, and some verses spoken by him so enraged 'Amr ibn Hind, the King of Ḥíra (A.D. 554–569), that he sent Ṭarafa to the governor of Baḥrain with a sealed letter containing orders to kill him. The following lines from his *Mu'allaḳa* illustrate the pre-Islamic view of life as well as the character of the poet who was cut off in the flower of his days.

8

Canst thou make me immortal, O thou that blamest me so
For haunting the battle and loving the pleasures that fly?
If thou hast not the power to ward me from Death, let me go
To meet him and scatter the wealth in my hand, ere I die.

Save only for three things in which noble youth take delight,
I care not how soon rises o'er me the coronach loud:
Wine that foams when the water is poured on it, ruddy, not
    bright,
Dark wine that I quaff stol'n away from the cavilling crowd;

And then my fierce charge to the rescue on back of a mare
Wide-stepping as wolf I have startled where thirsty he cowers;
And third, the day-long with a lass in her tent of goat's hair
To hear the wild rain and beguile of their slowness the hours[1].

'Amr son of Kulthúm

Chief of the tribe of Taghlib. In his *Mu'allaka* he addresses 'Amr ibn Hind, the King of Ḥíra, in terms of defiance and warns the foes of Taghlib that they will meet more than their match.

9

Up, maiden! Fetch the morning-drink and spare not
    The wine of Andarín,
Clear wine that takes a saffron hue when water
    Is mingled warm therein.
The lover tasting it forgets his passion,
    His heart is eased of pain;
The stingy miser, as he lifts the goblet,
    Regardeth not his gain.
Pass round from left to right! Why lett'st thou, maiden,
    Me and my comrades thirst?

[1] For the translation of this verse I am indebted to Mr Wilfrid Scawen Blunt, in whose beautiful version of the *Mu'allakát* it is rendered thus:
"And third, to lie the day-long, while wild clouds are wildering, close in her tent of goat's hair, the dearest beloved of me."

Yet am I, whom thou wilt not serve this morning,
Of us three not the worst!
Many a cup in Baalbec and Damascus
And Ḳáṣirín I drained,
Howbeit we, ordained to death, shall one day
Meet death, to us ordained.

* * * * *

And oh, my love and yearning when at nightfall
I saw her camels haste,
Until sharp peaks uptowered like serried swordblades
And me Yamáma faced[1]!
Such grief no mother-camel feels, bemoaning
Her young one lost, nor she,
The grey-haired woman whose hard fate hath left her
Of nine sons graves thrice three.

* * * * *

Father of Hind[2], take heed and ere thou movest
Rashly against us, learn
That still our banners go down white to battle
And home blood-red return.
And many a chief bediadem'd, the champion
Of the outlaws of the land,
Have we o'erthrown and stripped him, whilst around him
Fast-reined the horses stand.
Our neighbours lopped like thorn-trees, snarls in terror
Of us the demon-hound[3];
Never we try our handmill on the foemen
But surely they are ground.
We are the heirs of glory, all Ma'add knows[4],
Our lances it defend,
And when the tent-pole tumbles in the foray,
Trust us to save our friend!

* * * * *

[1] Here the poet describes his grief at the departure of his beloved, whom he sees in imagination reaching her journey's end in distant Yamáma.

[2] Hind was the name of 'Amr's mother and also of his daughter.

[3] Even the *Jinn* (spirits) stand in awe of us.

[4] Ma'add signifies the Arabs in general, excluding Yemen.

O 'Amr, what mean'st thou? Are we, we of Taghlib,
Thy princeling's retinue?
O 'Amr, what mean'st thou, rating us and hearkening
To tale-bearers untrue?
O 'Amr, ere thee full many a time our spear-shaft
Hath baffled foes to bow:
Nipped in the vice, it kicks like a wild camel
That will no touch allow—
Like a wild camel, so it creaks in bending
And splits the bender's brow!

* * * * *

Well know, when our tents rise along their valleys,
The men of every clan
That we give death to them that durst attempt us,
To friends what food we can;
That staunchly we maintain a cause we cherish,
Camp where we choose to ride,
Nor will we aught of peace, when we are angered,
Till we be satisfied.
We keep our vassals safe and sound, but rebels
We soon force to their knees;
And if we reach a well, we drink pure water,
Others the muddy lees.
Ours is the earth and all thereon: when *we* strike,
There needs no second blow;
Kings lay before the new-weaned boy of Taghlib
Their heads in homage low.
We are called oppressors, being none, but shortly
A true name shall it be[1]!
We have so filled the earth, 'tis narrow for us,
And with our ships the sea!

ZUHAIR

THE War of Dáḥis was between the tribes of 'Abs and Dhubyán. After it had continued for many years, two chieftains of Dhubyán —Harim son of Sinán and Ḥárith son of 'Auf—paid over to the

[1] *I.e.* we will show our enemies that we cannot be defied with impunity.

'Absites the sum of blood-money to which they were entitled on account of the greater number who had fallen on their side; and so peace was concluded. The *Mu'allaḳa* of Zuhair celebrates this act of munificence and urges the tribesmen to forgive and forget.

10

Noble pair of Ghaiẓ ibn Murra[1], well ye laboured to restore
Ties of kindred hewn asunder by the bloody strokes of war.
Witness now mine oath the ancient House[2] in Mecca's hallowed bound,
Which its builders of Ḳuraish and Jurhum solemnly went round[3],
That in hard or easy issue never wanting were ye found!
Peace ye gave to 'Abs and Dhubyán, when each fell by other's hand
And the evil fumes they pestled up between them filled the land.

* * * * *

Will ye hide from God the guilt ye dare not unto Him disclose?
Verily, what thing soever ye would hide from God, He knows.
Either meanwhile 'tis laid by within a scroll and treasured there
For the day of retribution, or avenged all unaware.
War ye have known and war have tasted, not by hearsay are ye wise:
Raise no more the hideous monster! If ye let her raven, she cries
Ravenously for blood and crushes like a mill-stone all below,
And from her twin-conceiving womb she brings forth woe on woe.

* * * * *

I am weary of life's burden: well a man may weary be
After eighty years, and this much now is manifest to me:
Death is like a night-blind camel stumbling on: the smitten die,
And the others wax in age and weakness whom he goeth by.

[1] Ancestor of Harim and Ḥárith. [2] The Ka'ba.
[3] This refers to the religious circumambulation (*ṭawáf*).

What to-day is passing, that I know, and yesterday what passed,
But the fortune of to-morrow I am blind and cannot cast.
He that deals with folk unkindly and would spurn them, underneath
They will trample him and make him feel the sharpness of their teeth.
He that hath enough and over and is niggard of his pelf
Will be hated of his people and left free to praise himself.
He alone who with fair actions ever fortifies his fame
Wins it fully: shame will find him out unless he shrink from shame.
He that for his cistern's guarding trusts not in his own stout arm
Sees it ruined: he must harm his foe or he must suffer harm.
He that fears the bridge of death across it at the last is driven,
Though he span as with a ladder all the space 'twixt earth and heaven.

Labíd

Labíd witnessed the coming of the Prophet and accepted Islam, but his poems (in which a religious feeling often shows itself) belong to the time when he was still a heathen. Being the work of "a true desert dweller," they have a freshness and delicacy that owe as much to nature as to art. From the opening verses of his *Mu'allaḳa*, translated in No. 11, readers can see how a typical Arabian ode begins: almost invariably the prelude recalls a love-romance and describes its scene—the spot where the bard's mistress had once camped with her folk until they again set forth on their wanderings.

11

(Metre: *Kámil.*)

Waste lies the land: they are gone who lighted and dwelt awhile
In Minà—all desolate now: Rijám and Ghaul are lone.
And the slopes of Raiyán, bare are they: not a sign of man
But is weather-worn as the writing scored on the broad flagstones.

Dim relics: over them, since the sojourners knew them, rolled
Of years a many in war and pleasure and holy peace.
With the stars' spring-rains they were blessed abundantly: thunder-clouds
Gushed down in floods on them, followed next by the drizzling falls—
Ay, clouds of night-time, clouds of morning, and clouds of eve,
Spreading darkness wide and afar and answering boom with boom.
Here flowers the rocket, and here the ostrich and antelope,
'Tis so wild and still, on the wadi sides bring forth their young;
And gazelles large-eyed stand quiet over the suckling fawns,
While around them gather in troops the weaned ones, free to stray.
O'er the dust-grey camp have the torrents swept and have limned it plain
As a scroll just fresh from the pen, its lines all fair and new;
Or as traceries on a woman's wrist, a tattoo of rings:
Pricked in with powdery soot the pattern sticks off distinct.
And I stopped to ask whither gone are they?—what avails to ask
Things hard of hearing and dark of speech that abide unchanged?

12

(Metre: *Wáfir.*)

So made I an end. When cares pressed thick upon me,
And love turned backward after the tryst and meeting,
I severed the cords thereof and away I wandered
On camel so fleet and strong she could ne'er be weary:
A stark beast—high she tosses her pair of riders—
Yet shrunken and worn with me on and off the saddle:
She stands as a castle built by a master-builder
Of Hájir with stones alike, each fitted squarely.
A wild-bull she[1], a brisk one, on whom the night-long
It rained in a pebbly upland, in Burḳa Wáḥif;

[1] He compares his camel, for her speed, to a "wild-bull," *i.e.* an oryx, which he proceeds to describe.

Who strayed from his herd, and storm-clouds entertained him
With big drops plashing, driven as the north-wind listed:
He shelters in brakes of thorn and in lotus thickets,
Alone as the hermit vowed to fulfil a penance;
And when on his back the soaked boughs drip their burden,
He moves to and fro his horn, head and shoulder stooping,
As though 'twere a smith bent over the work before him,
To burnish away rust-stains on the sword of iron.
With sunrise comes the pack on him, lop-eared buckhounds,
The eagerest running swiftly beside the horsemen.
He wheels, not in craven flight, but as oft in honour
A proud knight turns at bay and hies on to battle;
And Mulḥam is down, the rest beaten off, and crimson
The flanks of Ṭiḥál the brach, for the bull hath gored her:
With many a slanting thrust of his horn he riddles
Her side as a cobbler's awl rips through the shoe-soles.
Then quits he the field, the rain-floods ebbing round him:
He goes like a race-horse covered with cloths, no faster,
And makes for a winding gully; and now he ambles,
And now he puts forth the utmost of speed, unsparing:
His fore-feet cleave the shrub-sown sands of Dahná
As players for stakes who rummage amidst a sand-heap[1].
He crosses the plain, alone, in his morning glory,
As bright as the blade of sword that is newly polished.

(Metre: *Ṭawíl.*) 13

O Maiya, arise amidst the keeners and wail for him
That built for himself renown, a man that was loved and feared!
And cry unto God, "Oh, take not Arbad afar from us[2],"
And shatter thy grief-riven heart with mention of his dear name.
A stout pillar to his folk: they leaned on him: then came Doom,
And one day they marked for him a place in the earth to lie.

[1] This refers to the game called *faydl* or *fiydl* in which a heap of sand, after something had been hidden in it, was divided into two portions; then one player asked the other to guess which portion contained the thing that had been hidden.

[2] Maiya was Labíd's daughter, Arbad his brother.

14

O maiden, weep for Arbad wherever his clanfolk meet,
For he was the stranger's lodging and the starveling's safe retreat,
Our stay on a sunless winter day when rushed from the north a storm
And the gamblers shared their gains, while cowered in their shielings the churls wrapt warm.

(Metre: *Ṭawíl.*) 15

What here will a man devise to seek after? Ask him ye!
A vow that he may fulfil? or some idle errant thought?
The snares on his path are spread, encompassing him: if he
Unstricken escape the snares, yet soon shall his strength be naught.

He journeys the whole night long and saith in his heart, "'Tis done,"
Albeit a living man is ne'er done with toil and pain.
Say ye, when he portions out what now he shall do or shun,
"Bereaved may thy mother be! Hath Time preached to thee in vain?"

TA'ABBAṬA SHARRÀ

THÁBIT son of Jábir, nicknamed Ta'abbaṭa Sharrà, was a brigand and outlaw who lived in the last decades before Islam. Both he and his comrade, Shanfarà, were excellent poets. The poem translated below is Ta'abbaṭa's masterpiece; there are versions of it by Goethe, Rückert, and Sir Charles Lyall. The author tells how he avenged his uncle slain by the tribesmen of Hudhail: he describes the dead man's heroic character, the foray in which he fell, his former victories over the same enemy, and finally the vengeance taken for him.

(Metre: *Madíd.*) 16

In the glen there a murdered man is lying—
Not in vain for vengeance his blood is crying.
He hath left me the load to bear and departed:
I take up the load and bear it true-hearted.

I, his sister's son, the bloodshed inherit,
I whose knot none looses, stubborn of spirit;
Glowering darkly, shame's deadly outwiper,
Like the serpent spitting venom, the viper.

Hard the tidings that befell us, heart-breaking;
Little seemed thereby the anguish most aching.
Fate hath robbed me—still is Fate fierce and froward—
Of a hero whose friend ne'er called him coward.
As the warm sun was he in wintry weather,
'Neath the Dog-star shade and coolness together;
Spare of flank, yet this in him showed not meanness;
Open-hearted, full of boldness and keenness;
Firm of purpose, cavalier unaffrighted—
Courage rode with him and with him alighted;
In his bounty a bursting cloud of rain-water;
Lion grim when he leaped to the slaughter.
Flowing hair, long robe his folk saw aforetime,
But a lean-haunched wolf was he in war-time.
Savours two he had, untasted by no men:
Honey to his friends and gall to his foemen.
Fear he rode, nor recked what should betide him:
Save his deep-notched Yemen blade, none beside him.

Oh, the warriors girt with swords good for slashing,
Like the levin, when they drew them, outflashing!
Through the noonday heat they fared: then, benighted,
Farther fared, till at dawning they alighted.
Breaths of sleep they sipped; and then, whilst they nodded,
Thou didst scare them: lo, they scattered and scudded.
Vengeance wreaked we upon them, unforgiving:
Of the two clans scarce was left a soul living[1].

Ay, if *they* bruised his glaive's edge, 'twas in token
That by him many a time their own was broken.
Oft he made them kneel down by force and cunning—
Kneel on jags where the foot is torn with running.
Many a morn in shelter he took them napping;
After killing was the rieving and rapine.

[1] Although the poet's uncle was slain in this onslaught, the surprised party suffered severely. "The two clans" belonged to the great tribe of Hudhail, which is mentioned in the penultimate verse.

They have gotten of me a roasting—I tire not
Of desiring them till me they desire not.
First, of foemen's blood my spear deeply drinketh,
Then a second time, deep in, it sinketh.
Lawful now to me is wine, long forbidden[1]:
Sore my struggle ere the ban was o'erridden.
Pour me wine, O son of 'Amr! I would taste it,
Since with grief for mine uncle I am wasted.
O'er the fallen of Hudhail stands screaming
The hyena; see the wolf's teeth gleaming!
Dawn will hear the flap of wings, will discover
Vultures treading corpses, too gorged to hover.

SHANFARÀ

HIS *Lámíyatu 'l-'Arab* (the Arabian Ode rhyming in *l*) is justly celebrated. It begins with a passage addressed to his kinsfolk, bidding them depart and leave him to consort with a few desperate bandits like himself:

17

(Metre: *Ṭawíl.*)

Arise, O my mother's sons, and breast with your steeds the night,
For truly the love I bear is kinder to some less kin.
'Tis all ready that ye want for going your ways aright:
The saddles on, girths tied fast, and moonlight to journey in.

And somewhere the noble find a refuge afar from scathe,
The outlaw a lonely spot where no fires of hatred burn;
Oh, never a prudent man, night-faring in hope or fear,
Hard pressed on the face of earth, but still he hath room to turn.

To me now, in your default, are comrades a wolf untired,
A sleek leopard, and a fell hyena with shaggy mane[2].

[1] It was customary for the avenger to take a solemn vow that he would drink no wine before accomplishing his vengeance.

[2] The poet appears to mean that he has three friends who resemble these animals; but it is curious, as Prof. Bevan remarks, that an Arab should compare his *friend* to a hyena.

True comrades: they ne'er let out the secret in trust with them,
Nor basely forsake their friend because that he brought them bane.

And each is a gallant heart and eager at honour's call,
Yet I, when the foremost charge, am bravest of all the brave;
But if they with hands outstretched are seizing the booty won,
The slowest am I whenas most quick is the greedy knave.

By naught but my generous will I rise to the height of worth
Above them, and sure the best is he with the will to give.
Yea, well I am rid of those that pay not a kindness back,
Of whom I have no delight, though neighbours to me they live.

18

Bury me not! Me ye are forbidden to bury,
But thou, Ummu 'Ámir[1], soon wilt feast and make merry,
When foes bear away my head, wherein is the best of me,
And leave on the battle-field for thee all the rest of me.
Here nevermore I hope to live glad—a stranger
Accurst, whose wild deeds have brought his people in danger.

KHANSÁ

AMONGST the Arabian women who have excelled in poetry, especially in elegiac verse, the first place belongs to Khansá. Her proper name was Tumáḍir. She flourished in the age of heathendom but outlived it. In the dirges which she composed on her brothers, Mu'áwiya and Ṣakhr, depth of feeling is united with a noble simplicity of expression.

19

Tears, ere thy death, for many a one I shed,
But thine are all my tears since thou art dead.
To comforters I lend my ear apart,
While pain sits ever closer to my heart.

[1] Ummu 'Ámir, *i.e.* "mother of 'Ámir," is a name given to the hyena.

20

(Metre: *Wáfir.*)

When night draws on, remembering keeps me wakeful
And hinders my rest with grief upon grief returning
For Ṣakhr. What a man was he on the day of battle,
When, snatching their chance, they swiftly exchange the spear-thrusts!
Ah, never of woe like this in the world of spirits
I heard, or of loss like mine in the heart of woman.
What Fortune might send, none stronger than he to bear it;
None better to meet the trouble with mind unshaken;
The kindest to help, wherever the need was sorest:
They all had of him a boon—wife, friend, and suitor.
O Ṣakhr! I will ne'er forget thee until in dying
I part from my soul, and earth for my tomb is cloven.
The rise of the sun recalls to me Ṣakhr my brother,
And him I remember also at every sunset.

KA'B SON OF ZUHAIR

HIS father was the famous poet Zuhair son of Abú Sulmà (see p. 10 *supra*). When his kinsfolk became Moslems, Ka'b retorted by satirising the Prophet, who thereupon condemned him to death. He embraced Islam, obtained a pardon, and recited the following ode in praise of Mohammed. The Prophet was so pleased with it that he bestowed his own mantle on the author.

21

Su'ád is gone, and to-day my heart is love-sick, in thrall to her, unrequited, bound with chains;
And Su'ád, when she came forth on the morn of departure, was but as a gazelle with bright black downcast eyes.
When she smiles, she lays bare a shining row of side-teeth that seems to have been bathed once and twice in (fragrant) wine—
Wine mixed with pure cold water from a pebbly hollow where the north-wind blows, in a bend of the valley,
From which the winds drive away every speck of dust, and it brims over with white-foamed torrents fed by showers gushing from a cloud of morn.

Oh, what a rare mistress were she, if only she were true to her promise and would hearken to good advice!
But hers is a love in whose blood are mingled paining and lying and faithlessness and inconstancy.
She is not stable in her affection—even as ghouls change the hues of their garments—
And she does not hold to her plighted word otherwise than as sieves hold water.
The promises of 'Urḳúb were a parable of her, and his promises were naught but vanity.
I hope and expect that women will ever be ready to keep their word; but never, methinks, are they ready.
Let not the wishes she inspired and the promises she made beguile thee: lo, these wishes and dreams are a delusion.
In the evening Su'ád came to a land whither none is brought save by camels that are excellent and noble and fleet.
To bring him there, he wants a stout she-camel which, though fatigued, loses not her wonted speed and pace;
One that largely bedews the bone behind her ear when she sweats, one that sets herself to cross a trackless unknown wilderness;
Scanning the high grounds with eyes keen as those of a solitary white oryx, when stony levels and sand-hills are kindled (by the sun);
Big in the neck, fleshy in the hock, surpassing in her make the other daughters of the sire;
Thick-necked, full-cheeked, robust, male-like, her flanks wide, her front (tall) as a milestone;
Whose tortoise-shell skin is not pierced at last even by a lean (hungry) tick on the outside of her back;
A hardy beast whose brother is her sire by a noble dam, and her sire's brother is her dam's brother; a long-necked one and nimble.
The *ḳurád*[1] crawls over her: then her smooth breast and flanks cause it to slip off.
Onager-like is she; her side slabbed with firm flesh, her elbow-joint[2] far removed from the ribs;

[1] A large species of tick.
[2] *I.e.* the middle joint of the foreleg.

Her nose aquiline; in her generous ears are signs of breeding plain for the expert to see, and in her cheeks smoothness.
Her muzzle juts out from her eyes and throat, as though it were a pick-axe.
She lets a tail like a leafless palm-branch with small tufts of hair hang down over a sharp-edged (unrounded) udder from which its teats do not take away (milk) little by little[1].
Though she be not trying, she races along on light slender feet that skim the ground as they fall,
With tawny hock-tendons—feet that leave the gravel scattered and are not shod so that they should be kept safe from the blackness of the heaped stones.
The swift movement of her forelegs, when she sweats and the mirage enfolds the hills—
On a day when the chameleon basks in some high spot until its exposed part is baked as in fire,
And, the grey cicalas having begun to hop on the gravel, the camel-driver bids his companions take the siesta—
Resembles the beating of hand on hand by a bereaved grey-haired woman who rises to lament and is answered by those who have lost many a child,
One wailing shrilly, her arms weak, who had no understanding when news was brought of the death of her unwedded son:
She tears her breast with her hands, while her tunic is rent in pieces from her collar-bones.
The fools walk on both sides of my camel, saying, "Verily, O grandson of Abú Sulmà, thou art as good as slain[2]";
And every friend of whom I was hopeful said, "I will not help thee out: I am too busy to mind thee."
I said, "Let me go my way, may ye have no father! for whatever the Merciful hath decreed shall be done[3].
Every son of woman, long though his safety be, one day is borne upon a gibbous bier."

[1] *I.e.* she is a camel for riding, not for milking.

[2] Referring to his journey to the Prophet, who had already given the order for his death.

[3] "The Merciful" (*al-Raḥmán*), *i.e.* God. The word is Koranic, and by using it Ka'b signifies that he has become a Moslem.

I was told that the Messenger of Allah threatened me (with death), but with the Messenger of Allah I have hope of finding pardon.
Gently! mayst thou be guided by Him who gave thee the gift of the Koran, wherein are warnings and a plain setting-out (of the matter).
Do not punish me, when I have not sinned, on account of what is said by the informers, even should the (false) sayings about me be many.
Ay, I stand in such a place that if an elephant stood there, seeing (what I see) and hearing what I hear,
The sides of his neck would be shaken with terror—if there be no forgiveness from the Messenger of Allah.
I did not cease to cross the desert, plunging betimes into the darkness when the mantle of Night is fallen,
Till I laid my right hand, not to withdraw it, in the hand of the avenger whose word is the word of truth.
For indeed he is more feared by me when I speak to him—and they told me I should be asked of my lineage—
Than a lion of the jungle, one whose lair is amidst dense thickets in the lowland of 'Aththar;
He goes in the morning to feed two cubs, whose victual is human flesh rolled in the dust and torn to pieces;
When he springs on his adversary, 'tis against his law that he should leave the adversary ere he is broken;
From him the asses of the broad dale flee in affright, and men do not walk in his wadi,
Albeit ever in his wadi is a trusty fere, his armour and hard-worn raiment smeared with blood—ready to be devoured.
Truly the Messenger is a light whence illumination is sought—a drawn Indian sword, one of the swords of Allah,
Amongst a band of Ḳuraish, whose spokesman said when they professed Islam in the valley of Mecca, "Depart ye[1]!"
They departed, but no weaklings were they or shieldless in battle or without weapons and courage;

[1] This refers to those Ḳuraishites who accompanied the Prophet in his migration (*hijra*) to Medina and are known accordingly by the name of *al-muhâjirûn*.

They march like splendid camels and defend themselves with blows when the short black men take to flight[1];
Warriors with noses high and straight, clad for the fray in mail-coats of David's weaving[2],
Bright, ample, with pierced rings strung together like the rings of the *ḳaf'á*[3].
They are not exultant if their spears overtake an enemy or apt to despair if they be themselves overtaken.
The spear-thrust falls not but on their throats: for them there is no shrinking from the ponds of death[4].

Maisún

Maisún was born and bred in the desert. Afterwards she married Mu'áwiya, the future Caliph, and accompanied him to Damascus. The last verse alludes scornfully to her husband, who was then governor of Syria.

22

A tent with rustling breezes cool
Delights me more than palace high,
And more the cloak of simple wool
Than robes in which I learned to sigh.

The crust I ate beside my tent
Was more than this fine bread to me;
The wind's voice where the hill-path went
Was more than tambourine can be.

And more than purr of friendly cat
I love the watch-dog's bark to hear;
And more than any lubbard fat
I love a Bedouin cavalier!

[1] Probably a hit at the people of Medina, some of whom had urged Mohammed to show the poet no mercy.
[2] David is described in the Koran (xxi, 80) as a maker of coats of mail.
[3] Name of a plant.
[4] *I.e.* places where draughts of death are drunk.

JAMÍL

23

Oh, that youth's flower anew might lift its head
And return to us, Buthaina, the time that fled!
And oh, might we bide again as we used to be
When thy folk dwelt nigh and grudged what thou gavest me!

Shall I ever meet Buthaina alone again,
Each of us full of love as a cloud of rain?
Fast in her net was I when a lad, and till
This day my love is growing and waxing still.

I have spent my lifetime waiting for her to speak,
And the bloom of youth is faded from off my cheek;
But I will not suffer that she my suit deny,
My love remains undying, tho' all things die.

THE BALLAD OF THE THREE WITCHES

AS'AD KÁMIL, the hero of the following poem, is one of the legendary kings who reigned in Yemen (Arabia Felix) during the pre-Islamic period. The reader will have no difficulty in believing that these verses were recited by a wandering minstrel to the hearers that gathered round him at nightfall. They are, of course, the work of a Moslem—probably a professional story-teller—and may be as old as the seventh century A.D.

24

Time brings to pass full many a wonder
Whereof the lesson thou must ponder.
Whilst all to thee seems ordered fair,
Lo, Fate hath wrought confusion there.
Against a thing foredoomed to be
Nor cunning nor caution helpeth thee.
Now a marvellous tale will I recite;
Trust me to know and tell it aright!

Once on a time was a boy of Asd,
Who became the king of the land at last,

Born in Hamdán, a villager;
The name of the village was Khamir.
This lad in the pride of youth defied
His friends, and they with scorn replied.
None guessed his worth till he was grown
Ready to spring.

One morn, alone
On Hinwam hill he was sore afraid.
His people knew not where he strayed;
They had seen him only yesternight,
For his youth and wildness they held him light.
The wretches! Him they never missed
Who had been their glory had they wist.

O the fear that fell on his heart when he
Saw beside him the witches three!
The eldest came with many a brew—
In some was blood, blood-dark their hue.
"Give me the cup!" he shouted bold;
"Hold, hold!" cried she, but he would not hold.
She gave him the cup, nor he did shrink,
Tho' he reeled as he drained the magic drink.

Then the second yelled at him. Her he faced
Like a lion with anger in his breast.
"These be our steeds, come mount," she cried,
"For asses are worst of steeds to ride."
"'Tis sooth," he answered, and slipped his flank
O'er a hyena lean and lank;
But the brute so fiercely flung him away,
With deep, deep wounds on the earth he lay.
Then came the youngest and tended him
On a soft bed, while her eyes did swim
In tears; but he averted his face
And sought a rougher resting-place:
Such paramour he deemed too base.
And himthought, in anguish lying there,
That needles underneath him were.

Now when they had marked his mien so bold,
Victory in all things they foretold.
"The wars, O As'ad, waged by thee
Shall heal mankind of misery.
Thy sword and spear the foe shall rue
When his gashes let the daylight through;
And blood shall flow on every hand
What time thou marchest from land to land.
By us be counselled: stay not within
Khamir, but go to Ẓafár and win!
To thee shall dalliance ne'er be dear,
Thy foes shall see thee before they hear.
Desire moved to encounter thee,
Noble prince, us witches three.
Not jest, but earnest on thee we tried,
And well didst thou the proof abide."

As'ad went home and told his folk
What he had seen, but no heed they took.
On the tenth day he set out again
And fared to Ẓafár with thoughts in his brain.
There fortune raised him to high renown:
None swifter to strike ever wore a crown.

* * * * *

Thus found we the tale in memory stored,
And almighty is the Lord.
Praise be to God who liveth aye,
The Glorious to whom all men pray!

Ṣafíya of Báhila

Date unknown. In these verses she mourns the death of her brother.

25

Two boughs, the fairest ever tree possessed,
We sprang and mounted from the selfsame root,
Until men said, "Long are their shoots, and blest
Their shade and sweet the promise of their fruit."

But Time, whose villainy will nothing spare,
Destroyed my dear one. He did us excel
As 'mongst the stars a moon more bright and fair,
And as a moon from forth our midst he fell.

Farazdaḳ

Farazdaḳ (died in A.D. 728) is best known as a satirist, but from the following poem we see that he could praise with dignity and effect, even when his feelings were not engaged. Ḥajjáj son of Yúsuf, the subject of this elegy, governed 'Iráḳ for the Caliphs 'Abdu 'l-Malik and Walíd. Ruthless in putting down revolt, he was execrated by all opposed to the Umaiyad dominion. Farazdaḳ, though himself a keen partisan of the 'Alids, does justice here to the great qualities of their arch-enemy.

26

(Metre: *Ṭawíl.*)

Let all weep for al-Ḥajjáj who weep for the Faith or one
That sold unto God his life in guarding the Moslem land;
And him let the orphans weep whose mother, with arms begrimed,
From Fortune in wasting years of famine hath naught left o'er.
For ne'er since Mohammed died have eyes flowed for any man
Like him or beheld his peer, excepting the Caliphs' selves;
Nor ever the like of him was laid for the earth to bear,
Nor written a name like his in letters announcing death:
So firm to beat back and rout the demon of Mutiny
When War shows her grinning teeth—a she-camel scabbed and old.
Nay, never I saw a day of heavier grief and woe
And fuller of hands raised up to wipe the o'erflowing eyes
Than that morn when al-Ḥajjáj was carried upon his bier,
Who many a burden used to shoulder and win safe through.
When news of his death was brought, the woman that oft let stray
Her flocks in the wilderness would fain keep them close in fold,
And cried to her slaves, "Fetch home the cattle and tether them,
For he that was wont erstwhile to shepherd our flocks is dead."

Ay, dead, he that shepherded the Faith for believing men
And smote with his Indian blade the head of its adversary.
And would they had been cut off, the hands that interred the son
Of Yúsuf, what time they cast the earth o'er the covering stones!
But how could ye as ye gazed—and he in his winding-sheet—
At last lay him down betwixt the sides of a hollow grave?
For did not ye know 'twas he, whom there ye were burying,
That ruled in his master's name the frontiers of empire far?
He healed with his Mashrafite good sword the corrupted Faith,
And rancorous hates that breed dissensions he purged away.
No money prevailed on him to alter the just decree:
His sentence a rope, whereof not loose were the strands or weak,
But woven from left to right, for firmness, and then made fast
In knots twisted well and tied securely behind the neck.
The army that stood beyond the River, the tribes called up[1],
On hearing the death of him, their captain, with one voice cried,
"Unhappy are we: alas, the Strength of our host is dead,
Whereby every heart in hour of peril was braced again."

Yet surely, if al-Ḥajjáj is dead, Abu 'l-'Áṣ's race
Of generous hawk-like chiefs are living and have not died;
And never there failed Marwán a proud scion of his House,
A man perfect as the moon at full and without eclipse,
Who filled with his glory's light the region of al-'Iráķ,
And no one his vengeance feared except for his own ill deed[2].

Abú Nuwás

Abú Nuwás, who drank and jested with the Caliph Hárún al-Rashíd, was a poet of extraordinary genius. In his wine-songs he portrays with an art almost Greek in its ease and directness

[1] "The River," *i.e.* the Oxus. The tribes called up are those which were enrolled after the decisive battle at Ķádisíya in order to complete the conquest of Persia.

[2] In these verses the poet flatters the reigning Umaiyad Caliph, Walíd son of 'Abdu 'l-Malik son of Marwán. Abu 'l-'Áṣ was Marwán's grandfather.

not only himself, as he lived from day .o day, but the luxury and debauchery prevailing at the court of Baghdád, where Persian manners had become fashionable. He often ridicules the conventions of Bedouin love-poetry and the rude monotony of life in the desert:

"Let the south-wind moisten with rain the desolate scene
And Time efface what once was so fresh and green!
Make the camel-rider free of a desert space
Where high-bred camels trot with unwearied pace;
Where only mimosas and thistles flourish, and where,
For hunting, wolves and hyenas are nowise rare!"

Although he treated moral laws and religious observances with contempt, his *Díwán* includes some edifying poems on asceticism. Perhaps these were composed in moods of disgust and disillusion. One who was cynically frank in describing his own vices is unlikely to have assumed a virtue which he did not feel.

27

Four things banish grief and care,
Four sweet things incline
Body and soul and eyne
To enjoy, if they be there:
Water, wine,
Gardens bright and faces fair.

28

(Metre: *Wáfir.*)

O Málik! I pray thee go for the wine full early,
And if it be dear to buy, then buy it dearly!
Bethink thee how once a grizzled old tavern-keeper,
Whose whiskers were black with blowing the tarry wineskin,
I called, as he lay where slumber had stolen o'er him—
His head sunk low, the left hand's palm his pillow;
And he at my cry arose with a start of terror,
And hastened to light the wick, and it flared, and straightway
His terror was flown: he had gotten a look of gladness
And gaily haha'd—a clatter of idle laughter.
When now by the flame my features were lit, he gave me
The greeting of love, asked many a courteous question;

And into his hand I counted a thousand dirhems
To lodge me a month, with freedom for either party.
I found in his pleasure-domes two noble virgins
Of family high and proud, and became their bridegroom.
'Tis thus I have ever lived and am living ever,
Away my religion goes and my wealth in armfuls.
As oft as we meet, I like what the law forbiddeth,
And never can bear to like what the law hath hallowed.

29

Youth and I, we ran a headlong race of pleasure,
No recorded sin but soon I took its measure.
Of the gifts of Time there's none to heaven nigher
Than when music wakes the string of lute and lyre.
O the girl whose song— I had it for the asking—
Oft at Dhí Ṭulúḥ rose where our tents were basking!
Make the most of Youth, it stayeth not for ever;
Let the wine flow round from eve to morn—one river!
Pour into thy cup a sparking ruddy vintage
That will melt to ruth the miser's hardest mintage,
Sought and chosen out of old for Persia's ruler,
Dower'd with twin delights of fragrancy and colour.
Seest not thou that I have pawned my soul for liquor,
Kissed the mouth of fair gazelle and foaming beaker?
'Tis because I know, full well I know and fear it,
Far apart shall be my body and my spirit.

30

Thou scolder of the grape and me,
I ne'er shall win thy smile.
Because against thee I rebel
'Tis churlish to revile.

Ah, breathe no more the name of wine
Until thou cease to blame,
For fear that thy foul tongue should smirch
Its fair and lovely name!

Come, pour it out, ye gentle boys,
A vintage ten years old,
That seems as though 'twere in the cup
A lake of liquid gold.

And when the water mingles there,
To fancy's eye are set
Pearls over shining pearls close strung
As in a carcanet.

31

'Tis the dawn, my brothers! Drink!
The birds have sung their matin song.
Wake! The cup complains of us
To the can for sleeping overlong.

Pure wine when the topers mix,
Joy is born, until you see
The staidest rocking in his place
In an ecstasy of glee.

32

Muṣallà is desolate, I tread the Dunes no more; desolate are Mirbadán and Labab,
And the mosque where chivalry and piety met, and the spacious courts and enclosures
Which I frequented, a tall stripling, until the grey patches showed on my cheek,
With some lively blades in their prime of youth and graced with culture.
Then Time made trouble, and they were divided like the people of Saba and scattered in far lands[1].
Alas, never will the world give me such comrades again, so admirable were they!
When I knew for sure that they were gone and would never return as long as I live,

[1] "Like the people of Saba," *i.e.* irretrievably. The Sabaeans were the ancient inhabitants of Yemen. According to the legend, they were dispersed by a great flood which burst the Dyke of Ma'rib and laid waste the land. See my *Literary History of the Arabs*, p. 14 fol.

I displayed a patience not displayed by any one before, and diverse pleasures shared me amongst themselves.
Thus it is: when I am afflicted by the loss of a dear brother, there is no tie of kindred between me and him.
In the spring I dwell at Ḳuṭrabbul, and I pass the summer in the villages of Karkh[1], whilst my mother, the vine,
Suckles me with her milk and shelters me with her shade in the flaming noon:
When the boughs droop, I am covered with an unpierced roof of spreading shade.
The doves that haunt it keep mourning like bereaved women chanting a dirge;
Their longing and mine breathe tremblingly together, as though we were stirred by one emotion.
I rose, crawling to suck as a child smitten with hunger,
Till at last I chose for myself the daughter of a kiosk[2], on whom the years and generations had tried their teeth,
And in the thick gloom of night I tore from her the fine-woven fringeless veil
Wrought by a rude craftswoman[3], for whom no tethering-cord or tent-rope is made fast and taut in the ground.
Then I bored her waist with the point of the awl[4], and the wine gushed forth like flame.
Goblets of silver and gold collected it for the revellers and set it flowing round to us—
Goblet and wine so nearly resembled each other, I wondered which of them was the gold;
Both are alike, yet with a difference: that is solid and this molten—
Some smooth, some engraved with pictures of Christian priests and crosses,
Priests reciting their Gospel: above them a sky of wine whose star-bubbles
Shine like pearls strewn by the reckless hands of maidens at play.

[1] Ḳuṭrabbul and Karkh are places in the neighbourhood of Baghdád.
[2] *I.e.* a wine-jar.
[3] The spider. Cf. Koran, XXIX, 40: "The weakest of houses is surely the house of the spider."
[4] *Ishfà* (awl), *i.e.* an iron instrument, elsewhere (XV, 10) called *bizdl*, used for opening the clay-sealed mouth of a wine-jar.

33

Ho! a cup, and fill it up, and tell me it is wine,
For never will I drink in shade if I can drink in shine.
Curst and poor is every hour that sober I must go,
But rich am I whene'er well drunk I stagger to and fro.
Speak, for shame, the loved one's name, let vain disguises fall;
Good for naught are pleasures hid behind a curtain-wall.

34

Come, Sulaimán, sing to me,
And the wine, quick, bring to me!
Lo, already Dawn is here
In a golden mantle clear.
Whilst the flask goes twinkling round,
Pour me a cup that leaves me drowned
With oblivion, ne'er so nigh
Let the shrill muezzin cry!

35

The lovelorn wretch stopped at a (deserted) camping-ground to question it, and I stopped to enquire after the local tavern.
May Allah not dry the eyes of him that wept over stones, and may He not ease the pain of him that yearns to a tent-peg[1]!
They said, "Didst thou commemorate the dwelling-places of the tribe of Asad?" Plague on thee! tell me, who are the Banú Asad?
And who are Tamím and Ḳais and their kinsfolk? In the sight of Allah the Bedouins are nobody[2].
Leave this—may I lack thy company!—and drink old yellow wine, coursing between the water and the froth,
From the hand of a boy with the girdle on his slender waist[3], a straight well-shaped lad and lissome as a willow-bough:

[1] Here Abú Nuwás derides the fashionable poets who generally begin their odes with a lament over the relics of a deserted habitation. Cf. No. 11.

[2] By this time respect for the traditions and ideals of the pagan Arabs had largely passed away under the influence of Moslem pietism and Persian culture.

[3] Jews, Christians, and Zoroastrians wore a girdle to distinguish them from the faithful. The wine-seller would, of course, be an infidel.

When his father saw that I was lying in wait for him, he greeted me and made sure that I would squander my money,
And brought me a vintage which he is in no hurry to fetch (for his customers) and will not sell without striking hands[1].
Be generous and give thy whole fortune for it: do not hoard anything to-day for fear of being poor to-morrow.
What a distance between the purchaser of a delicious wine and him that weeps over a ditch and dyke[2]!
O railer, there hath come to me a hasty word from thee: if my forgiveness cover it up, do not offend again!
Were thy blame sincere, I would accept it, but thy blame is chargeable to envy.

Abu 'l-'Atáhiya

If Abu 'l-'Atáhiya was inferior to Abú Nuwás as a poet, he took a view of life which appeals to the typical Moslem far more than that of his contemporary. Because his religious asceticism is tinged with moral philosophy, he was accused of being a free-thinker; but the spirit of his poetry is orthodox: he does not, like Abu 'l-'Alá al-Ma'arrí, suggest doubts and insinuate disbelief in the faith which he professes.

36

Get sons for death, build houses for decay!
All, all, ye wend annihilation's way.
For whom build we, who must ourselves return
Into our native element of clay?
O Death, nor violence nor flattery thou
Dost use; but when thou com'st, escape none may.
Methinks, thou art ready to surprise mine age,
As age surprised and made my youth his prey.
What ails me, World, that every place perforce
I lodge thee in, it galleth me to stay?

[1] *I.e.* without making a formal bargain.
[2] Bedouins dig round their tents a trench which, together with the banked-up earth, serves them as an aqueduct and also as a dyke.

And O Time, how do I behold thee run
To spoil me? Thine own gift thou tak'st away!
O Time! inconstant, mutable art thou,
And o'er the realm of ruin is thy sway.
What ails me that no glad result it brings
Whene'er, O World, to milk thee I essay?
And when I court thee, why dost thou raise up
On all sides only trouble and dismay?
Men seek thee every wise, but thou art like
A dream; the shadow of a cloud; the day
Which hath but now departed, nevermore
To dawn again; a glittering vapour gay.
This people thou hast paid in full: their feet
Are on the stirrup—let them not delay!
But those that do good works and labour well
Hereafter shall receive the promised pay.
As if no punishment I had to fear,
A load of sin upon my neck I lay;
And whilst the world I love, from Truth, alas,
Still my besotted senses go astray.
I shall be asked of all my business here:
What can I plead then? What can I gainsay?
What argument allege, when I am called
To render my account on Reckoning-Day?
Dooms twain in that dread hour shall be revealed,
When I the scroll of these mine acts survey:
Either to dwell in everlasting bliss,
Or suffer torments of the damned for aye.

37

Surely shall Fate disjoint the proudest nose,
All wears away by movement and repose.
In long experience if wisdom be,
Less than my portion is enough for me.
Eager I take the hopes my soul inspires;
False are these hopes and vain are these desires.
That my hereafter I neglect is clear,
Since I am pleased and happy with things here.

O thou that gloriest in thy worldly state,
Mud piled on mud will never make thee great.
Nay, wouldst thou see the noblest man of all,
Look at a monarch in a beggar's pall[1]!
To him great honour by the folk is given,
'Tis he knows how to live on earth for Heaven.

FÁRI'A DAUGHTER OF ṬARÍF

A dirge for her brother, Walíd the Khárijite, who was slain in battle by Yazíd son of Mazyad in the reign of Hárún al-Rashíd.

38

(Metre: *Ṭawíl.*)

At Tallu Nuhákà stands the cairn of a grave set high
As though on a mountain-peak o'ertopping the mountains,
A grave that doth hold renown most ancient and chieftainhood
And courage heroical and judgment unshaken.
But why bud ye, O ye trees of Khábúr, with leaves afresh?
Methinks, ye have never mourned Ṭaríf's son, my brother.
He liked not of food but that he gained in the fear of God,
Of wealth only what was won by good swords and lances;
Nor aught would he prize and keep but many a hardy mare
Sleek-coated, well-used to charge thro' ranks of the battle.
And now 'tis as though with us thou ne'er hadst been present here,
Or ta'en 'gainst our foes a stand not soon to be yielded;
Or ever done on, for sake of plunging in loathly fray,
A hauberk of mail amongst dark-glittering horsemen;
Or striven on a field of War, when big is her womb with woe
And keen tawny-shafted pikes have pricked her to fury.
The comrade of Bounty he, his life long: him Bounty loved,
And since he is dead, no more loves Bounty a comrade.
We lost thee as Youth, once lost, returns not; and fain had we
Redeemed thee with thousands of the lives of our bravest.

[1] Mohammedan ascetics and holy men are frequently described as spiritual kings (see my *Literary History of the Arabs*, p. 298, note 1). The metaphor, no doubt, is derived from the story of Buddha; but I do not agree with Prof. Goldziher, who thinks that in this passage the poet refers to Buddha himself.

For aye was Walíd, till Death drew right forth the soul of him,
A grief to the foeman or a home to the friendless.
Come weep, O my kin, the doom of death and the woeful
change
And earth trembling after him and quaking beneath us!
Come weep, O my kin, the turns of fortune, the perishings,
And pitiless Fate that dogs the noble with ruin!
Alas for the perfect moon fall'n low from amongst the stars,
Alas for the sun when toward eclipse was his journey!
Alas for the lion, yea, the lion without reproach,
What time to a hollowed grave, roofed over, they bore him!
Oh, God curse the mounded stones that covered him out of
sight,
A man that was never tired of doing a kindness!
If he by Yazíd the son of Mazyad was done to death,
Yet many a host he led of warriors to combat.
Upon him the peace of God abide evermore! Meseems
That fast fall the strokes of Death on all who are noble.

Ibn Hishám

The first biography of the Prophet was written by Ibn Isḥáḳ, who died at Baghdád in A.D. 768. The original work has been lost but is known to us at second hand in the recension of Ibn Hishám (died in A.D. 834).

39

Concerning the true visions with which the prophethood of Mohammed began

Ibn Isḥáḳ said: Zuhrí relates on the authority of 'Urwa son of Zubair that 'Á'isha told him ('Urwa) that when Allah desired to honour Mohammed and have mercy on His servants by means of him, the first sign of prophethood vouchsafed to the Messenger of Allah—may Allah bless him and give him peace!—was true visions, resembling the brightness of daybreak, which were shown to him in his sleep. And Allah, she said, caused him to wish for solitude, so that he liked nothing better than to be alone.

How the stones and trees greeted the Prophet

Ibn Isḥáḳ said: ʻAbdu ʼl-Malik son of ʻAbdullah son of Abú Sufyán son of ʻAlá son of Járiya the Thaḳífite, who had a retentive memory, related to me on the authority of a certain scholar, that the Messenger of Allah, at the time when Allah willed to bestow His grace upon him and endow him with prophethood, would go forth for his affair and journey far afield until he reached the ravines of Mecca and the beds of its valleys where no house was in sight; and not a stone or tree that he passed by but would say, "Peace unto thee, O Messenger of Allah!" And the Messenger of Allah would turn round to his right and left and look behind him, and he would see naught except trees and stones. Thus he stayed, seeing and hearing, so long as it pleased Allah that he should stay. Then Gabriel came to him with the gift of Allah's grace, whilst he was on Mt Ḥirá in the month of Ramaḍán.

How Gabriel, on whom be peace, came down

Ibn Isḥáḳ said: Wahb son of Kaisán, a client of the family of Zubair, related to me and said, "I heard ʻAbdullah son of Zubair say to ʻUbaid son of ʻUmair son of Ḳatáda the Laithite, ʻO ʻUbaid, tell us how was the beginning of the prophethood which was first bestowed on the Messenger of Allah when Gabriel came to him.ʼ And ʻUbaid, in my presence, related to ʻAbdullah son of Zubair and those with him as follows":

The Messenger of Allah would sojourn on Mt Ḥirá every year for a month, to practise *taḥannuth*, as was the custom of Ḳuraish during the Heathendom. [*Taḥannuth* is religious devotion. Ibn Isḥáḳ said: Abú Ṭálib said (in verse):

> "By Thaur and Him who made Thabír firm in its place, and by those going up to ascend Ḥirá and coming down[1]."

Ibn Hishám said: The Arabs say *taḥannuth* and *taḥannuf*, meaning the Ḥanífite religion[2], and substitute *f* for *th*, just

[1] Thaur and Thabír are mountains near Mecca.

[2] *I.e.* the monotheistic religion adopted by a few Arabs in the time immediately preceding Islam. See my *Literary History of the Arabs*, p. 149 fol.

as they say *jadath* and *jadaf*, meaning "a grave." Ru'ba son of 'Ajjáj said:

"If my stones were with the other gravestones (*al-ajdáf*)[1],"

meaning *al-ajdáth*. This verse belongs to a *rajaz* poem by him, and the verse of Abú Ṭálib to a *ḳaṣída* (ode) by him, which I will mention, please God, in the proper place. Ibn Hishám said: And Abú 'Ubaida related to me that the Arabs say *fumma* instead of *thumma*.]

Ibn Isḥáḳ said: Wahb son of Kaisán told me that 'Ubaid said to him: Every year during that month the Messenger of Allah would sojourn (on Mt Ḥirá) and give food to the poor that came to him. And when he passed the month and returned from his sojourn, first of all before entering his house he would repair to the Ka'ba and walk round it seven times or as often as it pleased Allah; then he would go back to his house. Now, in the year when Allah sent him, in the month of Ramaḍán in which Allah willed concerning him what He willed of His grace, the Messenger of Allah set forth to Ḥirá as was his wont; and his family with him. And when it was the night on which Allah honoured him with his mission and took mercy on His servants thereby, Gabriel brought to him the command of Allah. "He came to me," said the Messenger of Allah, "whilst I was asleep, with a coverlet of silk brocade whereon was some writing, and said, 'Read!' I said, 'I do not read.' He pressed me with it so tightly that methought 'twas death; then he let me go and said, 'Read!' I said, 'I do not read.' He pressed me with it again so that methought 'twas death; then he let me go and said, 'Read!' I said, 'I do not read.' He pressed me with it the third time so that methought 'twas death and said, 'Read!' I said, 'What shall I read?'—and this I said only to deliver myself from him, lest he should do unto me the like once more. He said:

'Read in the name of thy Lord who created,
Who created Man of blood coagulated. .
Read! Thy Lord is the most beneficent,
Who taught by the Pen,
Taught that which they knew not unto men[2].'

[1] *I.e.* "If I were dead and buried."
[2] Koran, *Súra* XCVI, verses 1–5.

So I read aloud, and he departed from me at last. And I awoke from my sleep, and it was as though these words were written on my heart. I went forth until, when I was midway on the mountain, I heard a voice from heaven saying, 'O Mohammed! thou art the Messenger of Allah and I am Gabriel.' I raised my head towards heaven to see (who was speaking), and lo, Gabriel in the form of a man with feet set evenly on the rim of the sky, saying, 'O Mohammed! thou art the Messenger of Allah and I am Gabriel.' I stood gazing at him, moving neither forward nor backward; then I began to turn my face away from him, but towards whatever region of the sky I looked, I saw him as before. And I ceased not from standing still, neither advancing nor turning back, until Khadíja sent her messengers in search of me and they gained the high ground above Mecca and returned to her whilst I was standing in the same place; then he parted from me and I from him, returning to my family. And I came to Khadíja and sat by her thigh and drew close to her. She said, 'O Abu 'l-Ḳásim[1], where hast thou been? By God, I sent my messengers in search of thee, and they reached the high ground above Mecca and returned hither.' Then I told her of what I had seen, and she said, 'Rejoice, O son of my uncle, and be of good heart. Verily, by Him in whose hand is Khadíja's soul, I have hope that thou wilt be the prophet of this people.'" Then she rose and gathered her garments about her and set forth to her cousin Waraḳa son of Naufal son of Asad son of 'Abdu 'l-'Uzzà son of Ḳuṣai, who had become a Christian and read the Scriptures and learned from those that follow the Torah and the Gospel. And when she related to him what the Messenger of Allah told her he had seen and heard, Waraḳa cried, "Holy! Holy! Verily by Him in whose hand is Waraḳa's soul, if thou hast spoken to me the truth, O Khadíja, there hath come unto him the greatest Námús[2] who came to Moses aforetime, and lo, he is the prophet of this people. Bid him be of good heart." So Khadíja returned to the Messenger of Allah and told him what Waraḳa had said. And when the Messenger

[1] The *kunya* or "name of honour" of Mohammed.

[2] *I.e.* Gabriel. In this phrase the word *námús* (*νόμος*) signifies "Confidant."

of Allah had finished his sojourn and returned (to Mecca), in the first place he performed the *ṭawáf* (circumambulation) of the Ka'ba, as was his wont. Whilst he was doing it, Waraḳa met him and said, "O son of my brother, tell me what thou hast seen and heard." The Messenger of Allah told him, and Waraḳa said, "Surely, by Him in whose hand is Waraḳa's soul, thou art the prophet of this people. There hath come unto thee the greatest Námús, who came unto Moses. Thou wilt be called a liar, and they will use thee despitefully and cast thee out and fight against thee. Verily, if I live to see that day, I will help Allah in such wise as He knoweth." Then he brought his head near to him and kissed his sinciput; and the Messenger of Allah went to his own house.

40

The Battle of Badr

Ibn Isḥáḳ said: The men of Ḳuraish, having marched forth at daybreak, now came on. When the Messenger of Allah saw them descending from the hill 'Aḳanḳal into the valley, he cried, "O Allah, here come Ḳuraish in their vanity and pride, contending with Thee and calling Thy messenger a liar. O Allah, grant the help which Thou didst promise me. Destroy them this morning!" Before uttering these words, he had espied amongst the enemy 'Utba son of Rabí'a, mounted on a red camel, and said, "If there be aught good in any one of them, it will be with the man on the red camel: if they hearken unto him, they will take the right way." Khufáf son of Aimá son of Raḥaḍa, or his father Aimá son of Raḥaḍa, the Ghifárite, had sent to Ḳuraish, as they passed by, a son of his with some camels for slaughter, which he gave them as a gift, saying, "If ye desire that we aid you with arms and men, we will do so"; but they sent to him the following message by the mouth of his son—"Thou hast done all that a kinsman ought. If we are fighting only men, we are surely strong enough for them; and if we are fighting Allah, as Mohammed declares, none is able to withstand Allah." And when Ḳuraish encamped, some of them, amongst whom was Ḥakím son of Ḥizám, went to the tank of the Messenger of Allah to drink. "Let them be!" he said; and every man that drank of it on that day was killed, excepting Ḥakím son of Ḥizám, who afterwards became a good Moslem and used to say, when he was earnest in his oath, "Nay, by Him who saved me on the day of Badr."

How Ḳuraish took counsel whether they should return without fighting

Ibn Isḥáḳ said: My father, Isḥáḳ son of Yasár, and other learned men have related on the authority of some elders of the Anṣár that when the enemy had settled in their camp, they sent 'Umair son of Wahb the Jumaḥite to ascertain the number of those with Mohammed. He rode on horseback round the Moslem camp and on his return said, "Three hundred men, a little more or less; but wait till I see whether they have any in ambush or support." He made his way far into the valley but saw nothing. On his return he said, "I have seen nothing, but O people of Ḳuraish, I have seen calamities fraught with dooms—the camels of Yathrib (Medina) laden with slaughter and death. These men have no defence or refuge but their swords. By Allah! I deem not that a man of them will be slain till he slay one of you, and if they kill of you a number equal to their own, what is the good of living after that? Consider, then, what ye will do." When Ḥakím son of Ḥizám heard those words, he went on foot amongst the folk until he came to 'Utba son of Rabí'a and said, "O Abu 'l-Walíd, thou art chief and lord of Ḳuraish and he whom they obey. Dost thou wish to be remembered with praise amongst them to the end of time?" Said 'Utba, "How may that be, O Ḥakím?" He answered, "Lead them back (to Mecca) and take up the cause of thy confederate, 'Amr son of the Ḥaḍramite." "I will do it," cried 'Utba, "and thou art witness against me (if I break my word): he was under my protection, it behoves me to pay his bloodwit and what was seized of his wealth (to his kinsmen). Now go thou to the son of Ḥanẓalíya"—meaning Abú Jahl—"for I do not fear that any one will make trouble except him." [Ibn Hishám said: Ḥanẓalíya was the mother of Abú Jahl: her name was Asmá, and she was the daughter of Mukharriba, one of the Banú Nahshal son of Dárim son of Málik son of Ḥanẓala son of Málik son of Zaid Manát son of Tamím.] Then 'Utba rose to speak and said, "O people of Ḳuraish! By Allah, ye will gain naught by giving battle to Mohammed and his companions. By Allah, if ye fall upon him, ye will evermore look each one of you with loathing on the face of another who has slain the son of his paternal or maternal uncle or some man of his kith and kin. Therefore turn back and leave Mohammed to the rest of the Arabs. If they smite him, that is what ye desire; and if it be otherwise, he will find that ye have not sought to do unto him as ye desire[1]."

Ḥakím said: "I went to Abú Jahl and found him making ready a coat of mail which he had taken out of its bag. I said to him, 'O Abu 'l-Ḥakam, 'Utba hath sent me to thee with such and such a message,' and I told him what 'Utba had said. 'By Allah,' he cried, 'his lungs became swollen (with fear) when he saw Mohammed and his companions. No, by Allah, we will not turn back until Allah decide between us and Mohammed. 'Utba does not believe his own words, but he has seen that Mohammed and his companions are (in number as) the eaters of one slaughtered camel, and his son is amongst them, so he was afraid lest ye slay him.' Then he sent to 'Ámir son of the Ḥaḍramite, saying, 'Thy confederate ('Utba) is for turning back with the folk at this time when thou seest thy blood-revenge before thine eyes. Arise, therefore, and recall thy covenant and the murder of thy brother.' And 'Ámir son of the Ḥaḍramite arose and uncovered; then he cried, 'Alas for 'Amr! Alas for 'Amr!' And war was kindled and all was marred and the folk held stubbornly on their evil course and the advice of 'Utba was wasted on them. When 'Utba heard how Abú Jahl had taunted him, he said, 'He with the dyed breech will find out whose lungs are swollen, mine or his.'" [Ibn Hishám

[1] *I.e.* If Mohammed be victorious over the Arabs, he will have no reason for taking vengeance on you, who have not sought to destroy him.

said: *Saḥr* is the lungs together with the parts above the navel adjoining the windpipe; what is below the navel is named *ḳuṣb*, as in the Prophet's saying, which was related to me by Abú 'Ubaida, "I saw 'Amr son of Luḥai dragging his guts (*ḳuṣb*) in Hell-fire."] Then 'Utba looked for a helmet to put on his head, but seeing his head was so big that he could not find in the army a helmet that would contain it, he wound his head with a piece of cloth belonging to him."

How Aswad the Makhzúmite was slain

Ibn Isḥáḳ said: Aswad son of 'Abdu 'l-Asad the Makhzúmite who was a quarrelsome ill-natured man, stepped forth and said, "I swear to Allah that I will drink from their cistern or destroy it or die before reaching it." Ḥamza son of 'Abdu 'l-Muṭṭalib came forth against him, and when the twain met, Ḥamza smote him and severed his foot and half of his shank ere he reached the cistern. He fell on his back and lay there, blood streaming from his foot towards his comrades. Then he crawled to the cistern and threw himself into it with the purpose of fulfilling his oath, but Ḥamza followed him and smote him and killed him in the cistern.

How 'Utba challenged the Moslems to single combat

Then after him 'Utba son of Rabí'a stepped forth between his brother Shaiba son of Rabí'a and his son Walíd son of 'Utba, and when he stood clear of the ranks gave the challenge for single combat. Three men of the Anṣár[1] came out against him: 'Auf and Mu'awwidh the sons of Ḥárith (their mother was 'Afrá) and another man, said to have been 'Abdullah son of Rawáḥa. The Ḳuraishites said, "Who are ye?" They answered, "Some of the Anṣár," whereupon the three of Ḳuraish said, "We have naught to do with you." Then the herald of Ḳuraish shouted, "O Mohammed! Send forth against us our peers of our own tribe!" The Messenger of Allah said, "Arise, O 'Ubaida son of Ḥárith, and arise, O Ḥamza, and arise, O 'Alí." And when they arose and approached them, the Ḳuraishites said, "Who are ye?" And having heard each declare his name, they said, "Ay, these

[1] The men of Medina.

are noble and our peers." Now 'Ubaida was the eldest of them, and he faced 'Utba son of Rabí'a, while Ḥamza faced Shaiba son of Rabí'a and 'Alí faced Walíd son of 'Utba. It was not long ere Ḥamza slew Shaiba and 'Alí slew Walíd. 'Ubaida and 'Utba exchanged two blows with one another and each laid his enemy low. Then Ḥamza and 'Alí rushed on 'Utba with their swords and despatched him and bore away their comrade and brought him back to his friends. Ibn Isḥáḳ said: 'Áṣim son of 'Umar son of Ḳatáda related to me that when the men of the Anṣár declared their lineage, 'Utba said, "Ye are noble and our peers, but we desire men of our own tribe."

How the two armies met

Ibn Isḥáḳ said: Then they advanced and drew near to one another. The Messenger of Allah had ordered his companions not to attack until he gave the word and if the enemy should encompass them, they were to keep them off with showers of arrows. He himself remained in the hut with Abú Bakr the Ṣiddíḳ[1]. The battle of Badr was fought on Friday morning, the 17th of the month of Ramaḍán. Ibn Isḥáḳ said: So I was informed by Abú Ja'far Muḥammad son of 'Alí son of Ḥusain. And Ibn Isḥáḳ said: Ḥabbán son of Wási' son of Ḥabbán related to me on the authority of some elders of his tribe that on the day of Badr the Messenger of Allah straightened the ranks of his companions with an arrow which he held in his hand. As he passed by Sawád son of Ghazíya, a confederate of the sons of 'Adí son of Najjár—Ibn Hishám said: according to others, his name is Sawwád son of Ghazíya—who was standing in front of the rest, he pricked him in his belly with the arrow, saying, "Stand in line, O Sawád!" "Thou hast hurt me, O Messenger of Allah," he cried; "and Allah hath sent thee with right and justice, so let me retaliate." The Messenger of Allah uncovered his belly and said, "Take thy retaliation." Sawád embraced him and kissed his belly. He asked, "What made thee do this, O Sawád?" "O Messenger of Allah,"

[1] Abú Bakr, who afterwards became Caliph, is known by the name "al-Ṣiddíḳ," "the Veracious."

said he, "thou seest what is before us, and as this is my last time with thee I wished that my skin should touch thine." The Messenger of Allah prayed for him and said it to him.

How the Messenger of Allah besought his Lord for help

Ibn Isḥáḳ said: Then the Messenger of Allah straightened the ranks and returned to the hut and entered it, and none was with him there but Abú Bakr. And the Messenger of Allah was beseeching his Lord for the help which He had promised to him, and amongst his words were these: "O Allah! if this band perish to-day, Thou wilt be worshipped no more." But Abú Bakr said, "O Prophet of Allah, do not further beseech thy Lord, for surely Allah will fulfil His promise to thee." And whilst the Messenger of Allah was in the hut, he slept a light sleep; then he awoke and said, "O Abú Bakr, be of good cheer! The help of Allah is come to thee. Here is Gabriel holding the rein of a horse and leading it. The dust is upon his front-teeth." Ibn Isḥáḳ said: The first Moslem that fell was Mihja' a freedman of 'Umar son of Khaṭṭáb; he was shot by an arrow. Then, whilst Ḥáritha son of Suráḳa, one of the sons of 'Adí son of Najjár, was drinking from the cistern, an arrow pierced his throat and killed him.

How he incited them to battle

Ibn Isḥáḳ said: Then the Messenger of Allah went forth to the folk and incited them and said, "By Him in whose hand is the soul of Mohammed, no man will be slain this day, fighting against them with steadfast courage, advancing, not retreating, except Allah will cause him to enter Paradise." And 'Umair son of Ḥumám, one of the sons of Salima, was eating some dates which he had in his hand. "*Bakh! bakh!*" said he, "is there nothing between me and Paradise save to be killed by these men?" He flung the dates from his hand, seized his sword, and fought against them till he was slain.

Ibn Isḥáḳ said: 'Áṣim son of 'Umar son of Ḳatáda related to me that 'Auf son of Ḥárith—his mother was 'Afrá—said, "O Messenger of Allah, what makes the Lord laugh (with joy) at His servant?" He answered, "When he plunges into the midst of the enemy without a hauberk." 'Auf drew off the mail-coat that was on him and cast it away; then he seized his sword and fought the foemen till he was slain.

Ibn Isḥáḳ said: And it was related to me by Muḥammad son of Muslim son of Shiháb the Zuhrite on the authority of 'Abdullah son of Tha'laba son of Ṣu'air the 'Udhrite, a confederate of the Banú Zuhra, that when the warriors advanced to battle, Abú Jahl cried, "O Allah, bring woe this morning on him that more than any of us hath cut the ties of kinship and wrought that which is not approved! 'Twas he began it all."

How the Messenger of Allah threw pebbles at the unbelievers and put them to flight

Ibn Isḥáḳ said: Then the Messenger of Allah took a handful of small pebbles and said, turning towards Ḳuraish, "Foul are those faces!" Then he threw the pebbles at them and ordered his companions to charge. The foe was routed. Allah slew many of their chiefs and made captive many of their nobles. Meanwhile the Messenger of Allah was in the hut, and Sa'd son of Mu'ádh stood at the door of the hut, girt with his sword. With him were some of the Anṣár, guarding the Messenger of Allah in fear lest the enemy should make an onset against him. And whilst the folk were laying hands on the prisoners, the Messenger of Allah, as I have been told, saw displeasure in the face of Sa'd at what they were doing. He said to him, "O Sa'd! by Allah, methinks thou mislikest what the folk are doing." "Yes, by Allah," he replied, "O Messenger of Allah. 'Tis the first defeat that Allah hath let fall upon the infidels, and I would liefer see them slaughtered than left alive."

JÁḤIẒ

'AMR son of Baḥr, generally known as Jáḥiẓ ("the goggle-eyed"), a native of Baṣra, died in A.D. 869. His accomplishments were many and various. Besides giving his name to a sect of rationalistic theologians, he compiled a large number of volumes abounding in anecdotes and curious information of all sorts. The extracts

41 and 42 are from the *Kitábu 'l-Bayán*, a work on rhetoric; the others occur in his *Kitábu 'l-Ḥayawán* or "Book of Animals."

41

Abú 'Uthmán said[1]: We have related a portion of the sayings and speeches of the Messenger of Allah (Allah bless him and give him peace!) and have quoted some speeches of the early Moslems in full. Now we shall mention some detached sayings and repartees of men famed for eloquence and some exhortations spoken by the ascetics, and we shall direct our attention to those which are brief, not to those which are long, in order that the reader may be diverted rather than fatigued and wearied.

'Utba son of Abú Sufyán said to 'Abdu 'l-Ṣamad, the tutor of his sons, "Let thy first step towards the improvement of my sons be the improvement of thyself; for their eyes will be fixed on thee: they will deem that good which thou dost commend, and that evil which thou dost condemn. Teach them the Book of God, but do not force them to it lest they find it tedious, or let them neglect it, lest they leave it entirely. Then make them recite the chastest poetry and the noblest Traditions of the Prophet, and see that until they have mastered one branch of knowledge they proceed not to another, for cramming the ear with words is a cause of misunderstanding. Threaten them with my anger, but do not call upon me to correct them. Be unto them as the physician who does not hasten to apply the remedy before knowing the disease. Bid them shun conversation with women and learn the stories of the sages by heart. The better care thou bestowest on them, the more thou mayst ask and the more I will give. Do not trust that I will excuse thee, for I have put my trust in thy competence. Be unsparing in correction of them and, please God, I will not be sparing in my benefits to thee."

Ḥajjáj[2] used to dislike Ziyád son of 'Amr, of the tribe 'Atík; but when the deputation (from 'Iráḳ) came to the Caliph 'Abdu 'l-Malik and praised Ḥajjáj, who was present,

[1] Abú 'Uthmán is the author's *kunya* (name of honour).
[2] The famous governor of 'Iráḳ (died in A.D. 714).

Ziyád said, "O Prince of the Faithful, Ḥajjáj is thy sword which never becomes blunt, and thy arrow which never misses the mark, and thy servant whom no detractor can accuse of failing in his duty towards thee." After that, Ḥajjáj liked no man better than Ziyád.

Ghailán son of Kharasha said to Aḥnaf, "What will preserve the Arabs from decline?" He replied, "All will go well if they keep their swords on their shoulders and their turbans on their heads and ride on horseback and do not fall a prey to the fools' sense of honour?" "And what is the fools' sense of honour?" "That they regard forgiving one another as a wrong."

'Umar said, "Turbans are the crowns of the Arabs."

An Arab of the desert was asked why he did not lay aside his turban. "Surely," said he, "a thing which contains the hearing and the sight ought to be prized."

'Alí said—God be well pleased with him!—"The elegance of a man is in his bonnet, and the elegance of a woman in her boots." And Aḥnaf said, "Let your shoes be fine, for shoes are to men what anklets are to women."

'Abdullah son of Ja'far said to his daughter, "O little daughter, beware of jealousy, for it is the key of divorce; and beware of chiding, for it breeds hate. Always adorn and perfume thyself, and know that the most becoming adornment is antimony and the sweetest perfume is water."

'Abdullah son of Ja'far bestowed largesse of every kind on Nuṣaib Abu 'l-Ḥajná, who had made an ode in praise of him. "Why," they asked, "do you treat a fellow like this so handsomely—a negro and a slave?" "By God," he answered, "if his skin is black, yet his praise is white and his poem truly Arabian. He deserves for it a greater reward than he has gotten. All he received was only some lean saddle-camels and clothes which wear out and money which is soon spent, whereas he gave an ode fresh and brilliant and praise that will never die."

Mu'áwiya held an assembly at Kúfa to receive the oath of allegiance as Caliph. Those who swore loyalty to him were required to abjure allegiance to (the House of) 'Alí son of Abú Ṭálib—may God honour him! A man of the Banú

Tamím came to Mu'áwiya, who demanded that he should repudiate 'Alí. "O Prince of the Faithful," he replied, "we will obey those of you that are living, but we will not renounce those of you that are dead." Mu'áwiya turned to Mughíra and said, "Now, this is a man! Look after him well!"

42

In the name of God the merciful and compassionate. We shall begin, in the name and by the help of God, with some sayings of the devotees concerning asceticism and with some mention of their characteristics and their exhortations.

'Auf said on the authority of Ḥasan: "The feet of a son of Adam will not stir (from the place of Judgment) until he be asked of three things—his youth, how he wore it away; his life, how he passed it; and his wealth, whence he got it and on what he spent it."

Yúnus son of 'Ubaid said: "I heard three sayings more wonderful than any I have ever heard. The first is the saying of Ḥassán son of Abú Sinán—'Nothing is easier than abstinence from things unlawful: if aught make thee doubt, leave it alone.' The second is the saying of Ibn Sírín—'I have never envied any one any thing.' The third is the saying of Muwarriḳ al-'Ijlí—'Forty years ago I asked of God a boon which He has not granted, and I have not despaired of obtaining it.' They said to Muwarriḳ, 'What is it?' He replied, 'Not to meddle with that which does not concern me.'"

Ziyád, the slave of 'Aiyásh son of Abú Rabí'a, said, "I am more afraid of being hindered from prayer than of being denied an answer to my prayer."

Some people said to Rábi'a of (the tribe) Ḳais: "We might speak to the men of thy family and they would purchase for thee a maid-servant who would relieve thee of the care of thy house." "By God," said she, "I am ashamed to beg aught of this world from Him who is the lord of it all: how, then, should I beg it from one who is not the lord of it?"

A certain ascetic said: "Your dwellings are before you[1], and your life is after your death."

[1] *I.e.* in the world to come.

And Samuel son of 'Ádiyá, the Jew, said in verse:

"Being dead, I was created, and before that I was not anything that dies; but I died when I came to life."

Ḥasan son of Dínár said: "Ḥasan (of Baṣra) saw a man in his death-struggle. 'Surely,' he exclaimed, 'a thing of which this is the end ought not to be desired at the first and ought to be feared at the last.'"

Mujálid son of Sa'íd gives the authority of Sha'bí for the following words spoken by Murra of Hamdán. Mujálid relates that he had himself seen Murra, and that according to Ismá'íl son of Abú Khálid, who told Mujálid that he had never seen the like of him, Murra used to perform prayers of five hundred bowings in a day and a night. Murra would often say: "When (the Caliph) 'Uthmán—may God be well pleased with him!—was killed, I thanked God that I had no part in his murder, and I performed a prayer of a hundred bowings. Again, after the battles of the Camel and Ṣiffín, I thanked God that I had taken no part in those wars, and I added two hundred bowings. Then after the battle of Nahrawán[1], at which I was not present, I thanked God and added a hundred bowings; and when the rebellion of Ibn Zubair took place, I thanked God for the same reason and added a hundred more." Now, I ask God to forgive Murra, notwithstanding that we perceive no justification for some of his words, for you will not find amongst orthodox Moslems a single jurist who denies that it is lawful to fight the Khárijites, even as we do not find any of them denying that it is lawful to fight robbers.

'Umar son of 'Abdu 'l-'Azíz[2] was questioned concerning those who murdered 'Uthmán and those who deserted him and those who defended him. He answered, "God withheld my hand from that bloodshed, and I prefer not to dip my tongue in it."

Abu 'l-Dardá came to visit a sick man and said, "How do you find yourself?" "I am in fear of death." "From whom have you obtained all good?" "From God." "Why,

[1] In the battle of Nahrawán (A.D. 658) the Khárijites were defeated by the Caliph 'Alí.

[2] The eighth Umaiyad Caliph (A.D. 717–20).

then, are you afraid of Him from whom alone you have obtained all good?" And when Abraham was cast into the fire, Gabriel (on whom be peace!) said to him, "Dost thou want anything, O Friend of Allah?" "From thee, nothing," he replied.

It has been related to me that 'Umar son of Khaṭṭáb[1] (may God be well pleased with him!) said: "O people, there came over me a time when I was thinking that those who recite the Koran sought thereby only Allah and what is His to give. But now meseems that some of you recite the Koran, seeking thereby what is with men. Oh, seek Allah by your recitation and seek Him by your works! Well did we know you when the Revelation was coming down and when the Prophet—God bless him and grant him peace!—was in the midst of us; but the Revelation hath ceased and the Prophet is gone, and now I know you only by that which I say unto you. Look you, whosoever showeth to us good, we will think good of him and praise him for it; and whosoever showeth to us ill, we will think ill of him and hate him for it. Restrain ye these souls from their lusts, for they are eager in desire, and if ye restrain them not, they will speed you to the most evil end. Verily this Truth is weighty and wholesome, and verily falsehood is light and unhealthy. To abandon sin is better than to strive after repentance. Many a time hath one glance sown the seed of a lust, and the lust of a moment hath left a long grief behind."

Abú Ḥázim the Lame said: "I have found worldly wealth to be two things. One of these is due to me, but I shall never receive it in advance of its appointed term, not though I should demand it with all the might of the heavens and the earth. The other is not due to me: I have not obtained it in the past nor shall I obtain it in the future. What is due to me is withheld from others, just as what is due to others is withheld from me. For which of these twain's sake, then, shall I waste my life and bring my soul to perdition?"

Said Jesus son of Mary—the blessings of God be on our Prophet and on him!—"Verily the friends of God have no fear nor do they grieve. They are those who looked to the

[1] The second Caliph.

reality of this life when others looked to its appearance, and to the state hereafter that abideth, when others looked to the life that fleeteth away. They made to die thereof that which they feared would make their spirits die, and they abandoned thereof that which they knew would abandon them."

And seeing him go forth from the house of a harlot, they said, "O Spirit of God, what doest thou here?" Jesus answered, "The physician comes only to the sick."

And he passed by some people and they reviled him. Then he passed by others and they reviled him. And the more they spake evil, the more he spake good. A man of the disciples said to him, "The more they do thee evil, the more thou doest them good: it is as though thou wert setting them on against thee and inciting them to revile thee." Jesus said, "Every man gives of that which he hath."

43

What follows was related to me by Abú Shu'aib al-Ḳallál (the Potter), one of the Ṣufrites[1]. He said: The ascetics amongst the *zindíḳs*[2] are wanderers. They have substituted a wandering life for the practice of the Nestorians and Melchites, who never quit their cells, while the Nestorians often dwell in chambers dug in the ground. They always travel in pairs; if you see one of them, you will not look far before espying his companion. 'Wandering' (*siyáḥat*), as they regard it, consists in not passing two nights in the same place. While travelling, they observe four rules: holiness, purity, veracity, and poverty. 'Poverty' means that they eat only such food as is obtained by begging and is willingly bestowed on them: thus any guilt or sin connected with it falls on the giver who has earned it for himself. 'Purity' is abstention from sexual intercourse; 'veracity' to refrain from lying; 'holiness' to conceal any fault, even if they are questioned about it. Two of those men entered Ahwáz. One went towards the graveyard to satisfy a want

[1] A sect of the Khárijites.

[2] This name, which is commonly given by Moslems to the Manichaeans, seems to be applied here to the Buddhists.

of nature, and the other sat down near a goldsmith's shop. Meanwhile a woman came forth from one of the palaces with a small box containing precious stones. As she left the road to go up to the shop, she slipped and the box fell from her hand. There was an ostrich roaming to and fro, which belonged to the people of one of the houses in that neighbourhood. When the box fell, its lid came off and the contents were scattered, and the ostrich swallowed the largest and most valuable stone. All this was seen by the wanderer. The goldsmith and his lads sprang forward, collected the stones, and kept back the people with shouts, so that none of them approached the spot. On missing the jewel, the woman screamed. Those present made a thorough search and put their heads together, but the stone was not to be found. "By God," said one of them, "nobody was near us except this ascetic who is sitting here: he must have got it." So they questioned him. Now, he did not wish to inform them that it was in the ostrich's belly, for the ostrich would be slaughtered and he would then have had a share in shedding the blood of an animal. He said, therefore, "I have not taken anything." They searched him and carefully examined every article of his property and plied him hard with blows, until his companion came up and besought them to fear God. Then they seized him too, saying (to the other), "You have given it him to hide." He answered, "I have not given him anything." Whilst both were being beaten to death, an intelligent man passed by and heard from some of them what had happened. Seeing an ostrich roaming about the street, he enquired whether it was there when the jewel fell to the ground. "Yes," they said. "Then," said he, "this is the fellow you want." Accordingly, having compensated the owners of the ostrich, they slaughtered it and on ripping open its intestine discovered the stone. In that short time it had become reduced to something like half its former size, but the intestine had given it a tint which brought them a greater profit than they would have gained by selling it at its full weight, since the fire of the intestine is different from the (native) fire of the stone.

44

In the fly (*dhubáb*) there are two good qualities. One of these is the facility with which it may be prevented from causing annoyance and discomfort. For if any person wish to make the flies quit his house and secure himself from being troubled by them without diminishing the amount of light in the house, he has only to shut the door, and they will hurry forth as fast as they can and try to outstrip each other in seeking the light and fleeing from the darkness. Then, no sooner is the curtain let down and the door opened than the light will return and the people of the house will no longer be harassed by flies. If there be a slit in the door or if, when it is shut, one of the two folding-leaves does not quite close on the other (that will serve them as a means of exit); and the flies often go out through the gap between the bottom of the door and the lintel. Thus it is easy to get rid of them and escape from their annoyance. With the mosquito (*ba'úḍ*) it is otherwise, for just as the fly has greater power (for mischief) in the light, so the mosquito is more tormenting and mischievous and bloodthirsty in the dark; and it is not possible for people to let into their houses sufficient light to stop the activity of the mosquito, because for this purpose they would have to admit the beams of the sun, and there are no mosquitoes except in summer when the sun is unendurable. All light that is derived from the sun partakes of heat, and light is never devoid of heat, though heat is sometimes devoid of light. Hence, while it is easily possible to contrive a remedy against flies, this is difficult in the case of mosquitoes.

The second merit of the fly is that unless it ate the mosquito, which it pursues and seeks after on the walls and in the corners of rooms, people would be unable to stay in their houses. I am informed by a trustworthy authority that Muḥammad son of Jahm said one day to some of his acquaintance, "Do you know the lesson which we have learned with regard to the fly?" They said, "No." "But the fact is," he replied, "that it eats mosquitoes and chases them and picks them up and destroys them. I will tell you how I learned this. Formerly, when I wanted to take the siesta, I used to give orders that the flies should be cleared out and the curtain drawn and the door shut, an hour before noon. On the disappearance of the flies, the mosquitoes would collect in the house and become exceedingly strong and powerful and bite me violently as soon as I began to rest. Now on a certain day, I came in and found the room open and the curtain up. And when I lay down to sleep, there were no mosquitoes and I slept soundly, although I was very angry with the slaves. Next day they cleared out the flies and shut the door as usual, and on my coming to take the siesta I saw a multitude of mosquitoes. Then on another day they forgot to shut the door, and when I perceived that it was open I reviled them. However, when I came for the siesta, I did not find a single mosquito and I said to myself, 'Methinks, I have slept on the two days on which my precautions were neglected and have been hindered from sleeping whenever they were carefully observed. Why should not I try to-day the effect of leaving the door open? If I sleep three days with the door open and suffer no annoyance from the mosquitoes, I shall know that the right way is to have the flies and the mosquitoes together, because the flies destroy them, and that our remedy lies in keeping near us what we used to keep at a distance.' I made the experiment, and now the end of the matter is that whether we desire to remove the flies or destroy the mosquitoes, we can do it with very little trouble."

ṬABARÍ

MUḤAMMAD son of Jarír, a native of Ṭabaristán—whence the name Ṭabarí, by which he is usually known—passed the most part of his life at Baghdád, where he died in A.D. 923. He was a man of immense learning and industry, and his great historical work, the *Annals of the Prophets and the Kings*, extends from the Creation to his own day. It is not a critical history, but a collection of narratives related, if possible, by eye-witnesses or contemporaries and handed down to the author through a series of narrators. Divergent accounts of the same event are given in full without any attempt to combine them. This is exemplified by the passage translated below, which comprises a portion of the long and dramatic description of the fall of the Persian Empire and the triumph of the Moslem arms. The decisive battle was fought at Ḳádisíya near Kúfa in A.D. 637.

45

The Battle of Ḳádisíya

The following narrative was transmitted to me in writing by Sarí, who derived it from Shu'aib, who had it from Saif, who received it from Muḥammad, Ṭalḥa, and 'Amr with the chain of their authorities.

The people of Babylonia demanded help from Yazdajird son of Shahriyár and sent to him this message: "The Arabs have encamped at Ḳádisíya with every appearance of being bent on war. Since occupying the place, they have left nothing undone; they have laid waste the territory between them and the Euphrates so thoroughly that no living soul is to be found except in the castles; the animals and all food that the castles could not hold have been carried off. They have not yet forced us to surrender, but unless help come quickly we shall give ourselves up to them." The princes who owned estates on the shore of the Euphrates wrote letters to the same effect, supporting this demand and urging Yazdajird to despatch Rustam to Babylonia. The Emperor resolved to do so and immediately sent for Rustam. "It is my purpose," he said, "to send you on this expedition. The greater the peril, the greater the steps that must be taken to meet it. You are the bravest man of the Persians to-day, and you see well that the danger now confronting them is such as they have never faced since the House of Ardashír[1] reigned in the land." Rustam signified his readiness to obey and paid homage to his sovereign. "Now," said the Emperor, "I wish to look into your mind, that I may know what you think. Therefore describe to me the Arabs and what they have done since they occupied Ḳádisíya, and also describe the Persians and what they are suffering at the hands of the Arabs." "The Arabs," answered Rustam, "may be described

[1] Ardashír Bábakán was the first and Yazdajird the last king of the Sásánian dynasty which reigned in Persia from A.D. 226 to A.D. 652.

as wolves who found the shepherds off their guard and wrought havoc amongst the sheep." "It is not so," said the Emperor; "I asked you in the hope that you would give a precise description, so that I might encourage you to act as the case requires, but you have not spoken to the point. Learn from me, then, what the Arabs and the Persians are like. An eagle settles on a mountain to which the birds resort at night. They pass the night in their nests at the foot of the mountain, and when they peep out at dawn they see the eagle watching for them. Now, if any bird should go forth alone, he will swoop on it, so they are afraid to rise from their nests; and whenever one flies singly, the eagle snatches it. But if they all rose together, they would drive him away, or at the worst they all would escape except one, whereas rising in small parties they will be destroyed one after another. This is what the Arabs and the Persians are like. Act, therefore, accordingly." "O King," cried Rustam, "let me be! for the Arabs will fear the Persians so long as thou dost not provoke them to give me battle. I hope to preserve the royal House. Peradventure God may have aided us, and we may have hit upon the right strategy and tactics. In war, judgment and strategy sometimes avail more than a victory." The Emperor scorned his advice and asked him what remained to be done. "In war," said Rustam, "deliberation is better than haste; and this is an occasion for taking time. It will be to our advantage, and more grievous to our enemy, if we engage his armies in turn rather than inflict a single defeat on him." As Yazdajird obstinately refused to listen, Rustam set out and pitched his camp at Sábáṭ. Meanwhile frequent messengers came to the King with the object of inducing him to dismiss Rustam and send another general; and the people gathered about him in great numbers. Sa'd the son of Abú Waḳḳáṣ[1], having been informed of this by spies from Ḥíra and from the Banú Ṣalúbá, wrote the news to 'Umar[2]. Alarmed by the appeals for help which poured in, through Ázádhmard son of Ázádhbih, from the inhabitants of Babylonia, Yazdajird, who was a headstrong and obstinate man, cast prudence aside and ordered Rustam to move against the

[1] The Moslem general. [2] The Caliph.

foe. In vain did Rustam repeat what he had already urged. "O King," he exclaimed, "thy rejection of the right course has obliged me to extol and justify myself. I should not have spoken thus, had I found any way of avoiding it. Now for thine own and thy family's and thy kingdom's sake, I beseech thee in God's name, let me remain in my camp while Jálinús advances. If fortune be with us, well and good; if not, I shall be prepared to send forward another. Then, if we find no escape and all means fail, we shall resist the weakened and exhausted enemy with our whole strength." Yazdajird, however, was determined that Rustam should march.

What follows was written to me by Sarí, who had it from Shu'aib, who learned it from Saif, who received it from Naḍr son of Sarí al-Ḍabbí, whose authority was Ibnu 'l-Rufail, who was informed by his father that when Rustam had encamped at Sábáṭ and collected the implements and munitions of war, he despatched his vanguard, 40,000 strong, under Jálinús, bidding him proceed cautiously and wait for orders before making a rapid advance. His right wing he entrusted to Hurmuzán, his left to Mihrán son of Bahrám al-Rází, and his rearguard to Bairuzán. He sought to encourage the Emperor, saying, "If God shall grant us victory over the enemy, the way will be open for us into their country, and we shall keep them busy in defence of their native land until they consent to make peace or submit to the same conditions as before." But when Sa'd's envoys returned from their audience with the Emperor, Rustam dreamed a dream which he liked not, and he boded ill and was loth to march and meet the foe. Perplexed and hesitating, he asked the Emperor to let Jálinús advance, while he (Rustam) stayed behind to consider what should be done. "Jálinús," he said, "is as capable as I, although my name inspires them with greater terror. If he win the day, that is all we desire; if it go against us I will send another captain like him and we can count upon repelling the invaders, at least for a time; for so long as I am not defeated, the Persians will set their hopes on me and will be of good heart, while the Arabs will feel awe of me in their breasts and will not dare to attack, so long as I refrain from giving them battle; but if I engage them they will be emboldened for ever and the spirit of the Persians will be broken for ever." Then Rustam despatched his vanguard, 40,000 strong, and marched himself with 60,000, leaving 20,000 to protect his rear.

According to the written account which I received from Sarí and he, through Shu'aib and Saif, from Muḥammad, Ṭalḥa, Ziyád, and 'Amr with their chain of authorities, when the Emperor insisted on marching against the enemy, Rustam wrote to his brother and the chief men of his country as follows:—"*From Rustam to Bindawán, the satrap of the Court, the arrow of the Persians, who is the man to deal with any grave event that may come to pass; by whose hand God will shatter the mightiest host and subdue the strongest fortress—to him and those near him.* Put your castles in order and prepare and be prepared. The Arabs, as though it were under your very eyes, have pushed into your country and forced you to fight for your land and your children. My advice was to hold them in check and wear them out by delay till their fortune should fail; but the King refused."

A certain man, whose story was handed down by Ṣalt son of Bahrám to Saif, by Saif to Shu'aib, by Shu'aib to Sarí, and given to me in writing by the last-named, has related that when Yazdajird commanded Rustam to march from Sábáṭ, that general wrote to his brother in the aforesaid terms or nearly so, and that he added: "The Fish (Piscis) has troubled the water, and the ostrich-stars (in the constellation Sagittarius) are fair, and Venus is fair, and the Scales (Libra) are even, and Mars has disappeared. I doubt not but that our enemies will conquer us and gain possession of the countries adjoining us. And the most grievous thing of all is that the King has said, 'You will march against them, or assuredly I will take the field in person.' Now, therefore, I am going to march against them."

Sarí communicated to me the following narrative, having received it from Shu'aib, who had it from Saif, on the authority of Naḍr son of Sarí, who was informed by Ibnu 'l-Rufail, whose father told him that the man who encouraged Yazdajird to despatch Rustam was the slave of

Jábán, the Emperor's astrologer. This youth was a native of Furát Bádaḳlà. Yazdajird sent for him and asked his opinion concerning Rustam's march and the coming battle with the Arabs. The slave was afraid to speak the truth, so he lied to him. Rustam had much the same skill in astrology as the slave, and because of his knowledge he set out with a heavy heart; but the Emperor, being deceived by the slave, made light of it....And Jábán wrote to Jushnasmáh as follows: "The power of the Persians has departed, and their enemy has been made to prevail over them. The empire of the Magians is gone and the empire of the Arabs is come, and their religion is victorious. Do thou, therefore, obtain from them a covenant of protection, and let not the things now passing beguile thee. Haste! Haste! ere thou be taken captive." As soon as the letter reached Jushnasmáh, he went forth to join the Arabs and betook himself to Mu'annà, who was then at al-'Atíḳ with some cavalry. Mu'annà sent him to Sa'd, by whom, after he had obtained a covenant of protection for himself and his family and his vassals, he was sent back to Persia as a spy. He presented Mu'annà with a dish of *fálúdhaḳ* (a confection of starch, honey, and water). "What is this?" said Mu'annà to his wife. "I think," she answered, "that his poor wife intended to make *'aṣída* (porridge), and has done it amiss." "Bad luck to her!" cried Mu'annà.

* * * * *

What I am about to relate was given me in writing by Sarí; he derived it through Shu'aib and Saif, from Muḥammad, Ṭalḥa, and Ziyád—with whom Ibn Mikhráḳ concurs—on the authority of a man of (the tribe) Ṭai.

On the day when the cavalry were engaged, the horsemen fought from dawn to noon. As the sun declined, the infantry on both sides advanced to battle and fought with great noise and din until midnight. The night of (the battle of) Armáth was called the *Had'a* (stillness), while the night of (the battle of) Aghwáth was called the *Sawád*, which word signifies the first half of the night. On the day of Aghwáth at Ḳádisíya the Moslems were always confident of victory, and most of the Persian leaders fell. In the centre their cavalry turned and fled, while their infantry stood firm; and if the cavalry had not rallied, Rustam himself would have been taken prisoner. After the first part of the night was gone, the Moslems passed the remainder as the Persians had done on the night of (the battle of) Armáth, and from evening until they retired (to rest) they kept shouting the names of their clans. When Sa'd heard the shouts, he went to sleep, saying to one of his companions, "If they go on shouting, do not wake me, for in that case they are superior to their enemy; and if they cease shouting and the Persians also keep quiet, do not wake me, for then they are equally matched; but wake me if you hear the Persians shouting, for that will be a bad sign."

When the battle waxed hot in the first half of the night, Abú Miḥjan, who was imprisoned and in chains in the castle, went up to Sa'd at eventide and besought him to pardon and set him free. From Sa'd he got nothing but rough words, so he came down again, and approaching Salmà the daughter of Khaṣafa[1], "O Salmà," said he, "O daughter of the house of Khaṣafa, wilt thou do a kindness?" "What is it?" she asked. "Wilt thou set me at liberty and lend me the black and white mare? By God, I promise that if He save me I will return to thee and put my foot back in the gyve." "How should I do such a thing?" said she. Then Abú Miḥjan began hobbling to and fro in his chains and reciting:

(Metre: *Ṭawíl.*).

"'Tis sorrow enough for me that here I am left in chains,
Fast-bound, while against the foe our horsemen the lances hurl.
Whene'er I would rise, the iron galls me; and none may pass
The barred doors that hem me in and stifle the captive's cry.
And yet had I store of wealth and brothers a many once,
But now they have left me lone: no brother at need have I.
I vow unto God and will not break unto Him my vow,
To visit no more the booths of wine, if I go forth free."

Salmà said, "I pray God may guide me to do what is best. I am content with thy promise; but as for the mare," she added, as she loosed his chains, "I will not lend her to thee."

[1] Salmà was the wife of Sa'd.

Then she returned to her room. Abú Miḥjan, however, led the mare through the castle-gate adjoining the moat, and having mounted her rode on cautiously until, when he was in front of the Moslems' right wing, he cried "*Allah akbar*" and charged against the left wing of the enemy, brandishing his lance and sword between the two armies. According to my authorities the mare was saddled; but Sa'íd and Ḳásim state that she was barebacked. Then he returned by the Moslem rear to their left wing and, shouting the war-cry, charged the Persian right, brandishing his lance and making play with his sword as before. Then he returned by the rear to the Moslem centre, rode forth alone in front of the infantry, and once more charged the hostile ranks in the fashion which has been described. That night he pressed the enemy sorely. The Arabs marvelled at him without knowing who he was, for they had not seen him in the daytime. Some of them declared he was the first of Háshim's men or Háshim himself[1]. Sa'd, who with bowed head was gazing on his troops from the top of the castle, exclaimed, "By God, were not Abú Miḥjan in prison, I should say it is he and the piebald mare!" Some of the soldiers said, "If Khaḍir (Elias) takes part in battles, we believe the man on the piebald mare is Khaḍir." Said others, "Were it not that the angels have naught to do with fighting, we should have said he is an angel sent to bid us stand firm." They never thought of Abú Miḥjan or recognised him, because he was in prison that night. At midnight, when the Persians stopped fighting and the Moslems slowly withdrew from the field, Abú Miḥjan returned to the castle, went in by the gate whence he had gone out, laid aside his armour, and unsaddled the mare. Then he put back his feet in the irons, saying:

(Metre: *Wáfir.*)

"Well knoweth Thaḳíf, my clan—no need for bragging—
That we are their noblest knights and their deftest swordsmen;
The richest of all in mail-coats long and ample,
The stubbornest when our rival will stand no longer;

[1] Háshim son of 'Utba was approaching with reinforcements from Syria.

And we in the days of peace are their chosen envoys—
Whoso to the truth is blind, let him ask and learn it!
Naught knew they of me, that night at Ḳádisíya,
For never I told the troops I was out of prison.
Held back if I be, then sore is my trouble surely;
And if I go free, with slaughter I feast the foemen!"

"O Abú Miḥjan," cried Salmà, "for what cause did this man imprison thee?" "By God," he replied, "not for eating or drinking anything unlawful; but I was given to wine in my heathen days, and I am a poet: the poetry creeps over my tongue, and sometimes my tongue sends it on to my lips, and so my praise is ill bestowed, and that is why he cast me into prison. I said:

(Metre: *Ṭawíl.*)

'Friend, bury me, when I die, a stock of the vine beside,
That after my death its roots may moisten my thirsty bones.
And bury me not amidst the desert, for lo, I fear
Lest when I am dead I ne'er shall taste of it evermore.
I pray thee, spill o'er my grave a cup of the saffron wine!
Ay, me it hath captive ta'en who carried it oft along.'"

Salmà's anger with Sa'd continued through the evening of Armáth and the night of the *Had'a* and the night of the *Sawád*. Next morning she came to him and made up the quarrel and told him her tale and the tale of Abú Miḥjan. Sa'd called him into his presence and set him free. "Go," he said: "I will not punish thee for aught thou sayest until thou do it." "Truly, by God," said Abú Miḥjan, "I will never allow my tongue to praise any shameful thing again."

Mas'údí

Mas'údí, who died in A.D. 956, was a great traveller, an enthusiastic seeker after knowledge, and the most versatile and discursive of historians. The following extracts are taken from the *Murúju 'l-Dhahab*, an abridgement of his larger works which are all but entirely lost to us. The text of the *Murúj* has been published with a translation in French by Barbier de Meynard and Pavet de Courteille (Paris, 1861–77).

46

The Barmecides

When the Barmecides were appointed viziers by (Hárún) al-Rashíd on his accession to the Caliphate, they took entire control of the revenues, so that he could not obtain even small sums of money which he required. In the year A.H. 187 he destroyed the whole family. Opinions differ as to his motive. Ostensibly, it was because they seized the revenues and set at liberty a man belonging to the House of Abú Ṭálib whom the Caliph had placed in their charge; but the real cause is obscure. Various explanations have been given, and God knows best what they are worth. We shall put them down here, as they occur to us, after we have cited some characteristic anecdotes of the Barmecides in the days of their power.

A person well acquainted with their history relates that one day, when Yaḥyà son of Khálid was present, al-Rashíd received a letter from the post-master in Khurásán informing him that al-Faḍl son of Yaḥyà was neglecting his duties as governor in order to devote himself to hunting and other amusements. Having read the letter, al-Rashíd threw it to Yaḥyà. "My good father[1]," said he, "read this and write to your son a letter that will prevent him from behaving in such a way." Yaḥyà took the Caliph's inkhorn and wrote to al-Faḍl on the back of the letter as follows: "My dear son, may God keep thee safe and give me joy of thee! The Prince of the Faithful has learned with displeasure that hunting and amusements leave thee no time to attend to public affairs. Now return to what will do thee more honour; for a man's good or bad habits are the only means whereby his contemporaries know him. Farewell." At the foot of the letter he added these verses:

"Seek glory all day long, no effort spare,
And patiently the loved one's absence bear;
But when the shades of night, advancing slow,
O'er every vice a veil of darkness throw,

[1] "Al-Rashíd had so deep a respect for Yaḥyà that in speaking to him he always called him 'my father'" (Ibn Khallikán).

Beguile the hours with all thy heart's delight:
The day of prudent men begins at night.
Many there be, esteemed of life austere,
Who nightly enter on a strange career.
Night o'er them keeps her sable curtain drawn,
And merrily they pass from eve to dawn.
Who but a fool his pleasures would expose
To spying rivals and censorious foes?"

"Admirable, my dear father!" exclaimed al-Rashíd, who had followed with his eye every word written by Yaḥyà. As for al-Faḍl, after the letter reached him, he never quitted the mosque during the daytime until he laid down his office and returned from Khurásán.

47

The siege of Baghdád by Ṭáhir and Harthama, the generals of the Caliph Ma'mún

Amín now took from the treasury a sum of 500,000 dirhems, which he distributed amongst the new officers, and he also presented each of them with a vial of perfume; but gave nothing to the veterans. Ṭáhir, on being informed of this by his spies, entered into correspondence with the malcontents, alluring them with promises and inciting the subalterns against their superiors, and kindled their resentment to such a pitch that on Wednesday, the 6th of Dhu 'l-Ḥijja, A.H. 196, they rose in revolt. Thereupon Ṭáhir moved from Yásiríya, camped outside the Anbár gate, and laid siege to Baghdád. Fighting continued by day and night until both armies were on the point of exhaustion. The buildings and monuments of the city were ruined and food became excessively dear. It often happened that in the same family one was a partisan of Muḥammad (Amín), while another was devoted to the cause of Ma'mún: brothers fought against their brothers, and sons against their fathers. Houses were destroyed, palaces burnt, and valuable property carried off as plunder.

Meanwhile from the east Harthama son of A'yan despatched Zuhair son of al-Musaiyab al-Ḍabbí, who occupied al-Máṭir in the neighbourhood of Kalwádhà and levied tithes on the merchandise coming by boat from Baṣra and Wásiṭ; then he placed the catapults in position to bombard the city and encamped in the marshland of Kalwádhà and in Jazíra. This beleaguerment inflicted great suffering on the inhabitants, and a sortie was made by a force of vagabonds and others who had escaped from prison. They fought almost naked: every man had short breeches and a cloth wrapped about his waist; a helmet, which they called *khúdha*, made of palm-leaf fibre; and a buckler consisting of palm-leaves and rush-mats which had been tarred and stuffed with gravel and sand. Each company of ten was commanded by an *'aríf*, ten *'arífs* by a *naḳíb*, ten *naḳíbs* by a *ḳá'id*, and ten *ḳá'ids* by an *amír*. All these officers were provided with mounts according to the number of soldiers under their command: thus an *'aríf* had, in addition to his company of fighting men, several men on whom he rode; and similarly the chiefs of higher rank were mounted on naked men with bells and tassels of red and yellow wool on their necks, and harnessed with reins and bridles, while brooms and fly-whisks served them instead of tails. In such fashion an *'aríf* would ride to battle, in front of him his ten soldiers with their palm-leaf helmets and rush-mat bucklers; not otherwise the *naḳíb*, the *ḳá'id*, and the *amír*. Spectators would gather and stand watching these men fight against adversaries who were not only mounted on excellent horses but protected by cuirasses, hauberks, coats of mail, and brassarts, and armed with lances and shields of Tibetan hide. To resume our narrative, the "naked" ones defeated Zuhair, but were put to rout on the arrival of reinforcements from Harthama. The human steeds threw their riders, and the whole force was driven back into the besieged city at the point of the sword. They left a large number of dead; and amongst the slain were many who came to look on.

Amín, being hard pressed for money, caused the gold and silver vessels to be melted in secret, and paid his troops with coin struck from these. Nevertheless, Ṭáhir got possession of Ḥarbíya and other suburbs adjoining the Anbár, Ḥarb, and Ḳuṭrabbul gates. The war now raged in the middle of the western city, and the catapults wrought havoc between the armies on either side. A poet, known as Blind 'Alí, refers to this in the following lines:

"O ye catapult-shooters, all of you are without pity!
Ye care nothing for friend or enemy.
Woe to you! Know ye whom ye are shooting? The passers-by in the street.
Many a fair young woman of gracious mien and like a leafy bough,
One that never knew the difference between a curtained bower and a crow's belly,
Hath been cast forth from the world where she enjoyed a sheltered and pleasant life.
There was no help for it: she had to go into the street on the day when her house was in flames."

The Karkh quarter and other districts on both sides of the river were scenes of conflagration and ruin. The splendours of Baghdád disappeared. As the situation grew desperate, the inhabitants, leaving the streets and lanes where they lived, wandered from place to place, and panic seized all hearts. The struggle between the partisans of Ma'mún and Amín lasted fourteen months. Baghdád could no longer house its population. Mosques were deserted and public prayers abandoned. Such calamities had never fallen upon the city since it was founded by Abú Ja'far al-Manṣúr.

* * * * *

While Baghdád was thus a prey to faction, the plight of Amín and his supporters became more and more critical. A great battle took place in the western quarter in the district called Dáru 'l-Raḳíḳ. The slaughter was terrible: every road, street, alley, and lane was filled with corpses. Foe rushed on foe, shouting, "Hurrah for Ma'mún!" and "Hurrah for the deposed Caliph[1]!" All the houses were pillaged and fired. For any one who escaped from these horrors—man or woman, young or old—it was the greatest blessing and joy to reach the camp of Ṭáhir with as much as they could save: there they felt that their lives and property were secure.

[1] Amín.

One of the captains of Khurásán came to Ṭáhir. Seeing the naked unarmed men engaged in battle, he turned to him scornfully and said, "What can these fellows without arms accomplish when opposed to our valiant soldiers who are so well armed and equipped?" He drew his bow, fitted an arrow to the string, and stepped forth from the ranks. The challenge was answered by a naked wretch with a rush-mat shield in his hand, carrying under his arm a bag filled with stones and brickbats. As the captain shot, the vagabond covered himself, and every arrow pierced the shield or just missed. Those that found the target he plucked out and placed in a receptacle, shaped like a quiver, which he had fashioned in the shield; and he continued doing this until the captain, having no more arrows left, charged at him in order to deal a mortal blow. The vagabond took a stone from his bag and cast it and hit the captain's eye; then he smote him with a second stone, which almost brought him down from his horse. His helmet fell to the ground, and he only saved himself by flight. He retired, saying, "These are not men: they are devils."

Every day the fighting became more severe, both sides showing the utmost obstinacy. Of the troops defending the deposed Caliph (Amín) there now remained none but naked rapscallions with palm-leaf helmets and rush-mat bucklers. Ṭáhir, pressing his advantage, occupied one street after another, and as each passed into his hands, its inhabitants joined the victorious army. Meanwhile his engines of war wrought great destruction in the quarters that still held out. He then began to dig trenches in the houses, hotels, and palaces which lay between himself and the defenders. His forces were strong and encouraged by success, while their adversaries were falling back and being gradually weakened. When Ṭáhir saw what resolution the partisans of Amín displayed amidst the ruins, conflagrations, and carnage, he cut off their supplies from Baṣra and Wásiṭ and blocked all the roads. The result was that whereas in a street occupied by Ma'múnís twenty pounds of bread cost a dirhem, in a Muḥammadí[1] district a dirhem would purchase only one

[1] Muḥammad was the name of the Caliph Amín.

pound. The misery of the besieged inhabitants was increased by famine, and they despaired of relief.

* * * * *

The position of the dethroned Caliph was extremely critical. Harthama son of A'yan lay encamped in the eastern quarter, while most of the western was held by Ṭáhir, and Amín remained in the city of Abú Ja'far (Old Baghdád). He took counsel with his favourites as to how he should save himself: every one present gave an opinion and advised a course of action. "Enter into correspondence with Ṭáhir," said one of them, "and swear to him an oath which he can trust, that you will hand over your sovereignty to him: perhaps he will comply with your request." "Be thy mother bereaved of thee!" cried Amín; "I was a fool to ask thee for advice. Dost not thou see that this man will never be induced to act disloyally? If Ma'mún had depended on his own exertions and managed affairs according to his own judgment, would he have gained the tenth part of what Ṭáhir has gained for him? My spies have thoroughly explored his intentions, and never have I found him seeking aught but noble deeds, high fame, and good faith. How shall I hope to corrupt him by gifts of money and make him a traitor? Were he willing to recognise me as Caliph and attach himself to my cause, I should not care though the Turks and Dailamites declared war on me. I should feel as safe as Ziyád ibn abíhi[1] when the Azdites took him under their protection, on which occasion Abu l'-Aswad al-Du'ilí said:

'When he saw them assailing his vizier, and when after a long delay they moved against himself,
He came to the Azdites, dreading that which has no alternative; and the course taken by Ziyád was the best.
They bade him welcome and said, "Thou hast done right: now make open war on whomsoever thou wilt!"
Then he feared no more any foe in the world, even if his enemies had brought against him a power equal to that of 'Ád[2].'

[1] Governor of Baṣra under the Caliph Mu'áwiya. His parentage was uncertain, and therefore he is often called "ibn abíhi," *i.e.* "son of his father."

[2] The pre-historic inhabitants of Ḥaḍramaut in South Arabia. They are described as a people of gigantic strength and stature.

By God, I wish that Ṭáhir would consent. I would let him dispose freely of my treasure and surrender my authority to him and be well satisfied to live under his protection. But I know I shall not escape from him, not though I had a thousand lives!" "O Prince of the Faithful," said al-Sindí, "you have spoken the truth. Were you his father, Ḥusain son of Muṣ'ab, he would not spare you." "Harthama, then," exclaimed Amín; "but how shall we find refuge with him? *for the hour of safety is past*[1]." He made overtures to Harthama, who accepted his conditions and promised to defend him from those who would kill him. On hearing this, Ṭáhir was indignant, and his anger did not abate until Harthama promised to embark his prisoner at the quay adjoining the Khurásán gate and convey him to Ṭáhir's camp, with any other persons whom that general might desire.

On the night which Amín had chosen for his escape—Thursday night, the 25th of Muḥarram, A.H. 198—a number of his adherents known as "the vagabonds" (*al-ṣa'álík*), brave soldiers and valiant gentlemen, presented themselves before him. "Prince of the Faithful," they said, "you have no loyal friend and counsellor; but we are 7000 warriors, and in your stables are 7000 horses. Let every man mount his horse; then let us open one of the gates and ride forth from the city to-night. The darkness will prevent pursuit, and by morning we shall be in Jazíra (Upper Mesopotamia) and Diyár Rabí'a. There you will collect money and men, then march through Syria and into Egypt. You will find troops and money in plenty, and your cause will prosper once more." "By God," cried Amín, "this is the plan!" He adopted it and resolved to carry it out, but amongst his pages and personal attendants were spies who sent to Ṭáhir hourly reports of what was happening in the palace. Ṭáhir, therefore, got the news immediately. He heard it with alarm, knowing that the plan would be likely to succeed. Accordingly he despatched the following message to Sulaimán son of Manṣúr, Ibn Nahík, and al-Sindí son of Sháhak, who were in attendance on Amín: "Unless you deter him from this enterprise, I will lay your houses in ruins, ravage your

[1] Koran, XXXVIII, 2.

estates, confiscate your fortunes, and take your lives." They at once went to Amín and caused him to abandon the project.

As soon as Harthama's skiff arrived at the Khurásán gate, Amín called for his black horse, Zuhairí, which had white streaks on its legs and a white star on its forehead; and summoning his two sons, Músà and 'Abdullah, embraced them and drew their faces close to his own and burst into tears, saying, "I commit you to God's care. I do not know whether I shall ever meet you again." Then he set off, preceded by a torch: his dress was white and he wore a black *ṭailasán* (hood), which covered his head. When he came to the quay beside the Khurásán gate, the skiff was waiting. He dismounted and severed the hocks of his horse while Harthama, advancing to receive him, kissed him between the eyes.

Ṭáhir, informed by his spies of the Caliph's flight, had sent some men of Herát, sailors, and others in barges on the river. Harthama had only a few of his men with him. When they put off from the shore, Ṭáhir's fellows stripped and diving under the skiff upset it, so that all on board were thrown into the water. Harthama could do nothing but save his own life: he caught hold of a barge and clambered into it; then he returned to his camp on the eastern bank. As for Amín, he tore the clothes from his body and swam until he landed near Sarát at the quarters of Ḳarín al-Dairání, one of Ṭáhir's equerries. Here a groom, noticing that he smelt of musk and perfume, arrested the fugitive and brought him to Ḳarín. The equerry begged Ṭáhir for leave to kill him and was conducting him to his master when the order came. The last words of Amín were, "*We belong to God, and to Him we are returning*[1]. I am the cousin of the Prophet and the brother of Ma'mún."

48

The ass that died of love

The Caliph Mutawakkil said to Abu 'l-'Anbas: "Tell me about your ass and his death and the poetry which he recited to you in a dream." "Yes, O Prince of the Faithful: my ass had more sense than all the cadis together; 'twas not in

[1] Koran, II, 151.

him to run away or stumble. Suddenly he fell ill and died. Afterwards I saw him in a dream and said to him, 'O my ass, did not I make thy water cool and thy barley clean, and show thee the utmost kindness? Why didst thou die so suddenly? What was the matter with thee?' 'True,' he answered; 'but the day you stopped to converse with so-and-so the perfumer about such-and-such an affair, a beautiful she-ass passed by: I saw her and lost my heart and loved so passionately that I died of grief, pining for her.' 'O my ass,' said I, 'didst thou make a poem on the subject?' 'Yes,' he said; then he chanted:

'I was frenzied by a she-ass at the door of a perfumer.
She enthralled me, smiling coyly, showing me her lovely side-teeth,
Charmed me with a pair of soft cheeks coloured like the *shaiḳurání*[1].
For her sake I died; and had I lived, then great were my dishonour!'

I said, 'O my ass, what is the *shaiḳurání*?' 'This,' he replied, 'is one of the strange and uncommon words in the language of asses.'" Mutawakkil was delighted and ordered the minstrels to set the poem of the ass to music and sing it on that day. No one had ever seen him so gay and joyous before. He redoubled his marks of favour to Abu 'l-'Anbas and loaded him with gifts.

49

The Caliph Ma'mún and the Ṣúfí

According to Yaḥyà son of Aktham, Ma'mún used to hold a *salon* every Tuesday for the discussion of questions in theology and law. On presenting themselves, the divines and learned men of different sects were shown into a chamber spread with carpets. Tables were brought in laden with food and drink, of which they were invited to partake after having washed their hands; and any one who found his boots uncomfortable might take them off, or lay aside his *ḳalansuwa* (bonnet) if it were burdensome. When the repast was finished, servants fetched braziers of incense, and the guests perfumed themselves: then they left the room and were admitted into the presence of the Caliph. He would debate

[1] The reading is uncertain.

with them, in a manner as fair and impartial and unlike the haughtiness of a monarch as can be imagined, until sunset, when a second repast was served, after which they departed to their homes.

Now one day (Yaḥyà continued), whilst the Caliph was thus engaged, 'Alí son of Ṣáliḥ, the chamberlain, entered and said, "O Prince of the Faithful, there is a man at the gate, seeking admission to the *salon*. He is dressed in coarse white garments, tucked up." Knowing he was one of the Ṣúfís, I was about to make a sign that he should not be admitted, but Ma'mún said immediately, "Let him come in." The stranger, whose garb was of the fashion already described, advanced with his shoes in his hand to the edge of the carpet, where he stopped and cried, "Peace and God's mercy and blessings on you all!" Ma'mún returned his salutation, gave him permission to approach, and bade him sit down. "Have I leave to address thee?" he asked. "Speak," said the Caliph, "if you know that your words will be acceptable to God." "Tell me," said the stranger, "of this throne on which thou art seated: didst thou ascend it by agreement and consent of the Moslems, or by using violence and force to gain the mastery over them?" "I ascended it," replied the Caliph, "neither by agreement on their part nor by violence on mine. Before me there was a ruler[1] who directed the affairs of the Moslems and whom the Moslems suffered willingly or unwillingly: he appointed me and another[2] to govern the state after his death, and bound those Moslems who were present to recognise his act; further, he demanded the oath of allegiance to me and to my associate from the pilgrims in the holy house of Allah, and they gave it voluntarily or otherwise. My partner in the succession went the way which he went, leaving the sole authority in my hands. I knew that I required the unanimous consent of the Moslems in the East and West, but on reflection I saw that, if I entrust the state to their charge, the firm bond of Islam will be loosened, covenants upset, the empire dismembered, all thrown into confusion and disorder and civil strife: the laws of God Almighty will not be kept, no one will

[1] Hárún al-Rashíd. [2] Amín.

make the pilgrimage to Mecca or join in the holy war: the Moslems will have no government to unite and direct them, the roads will be cut by brigands, the weak oppressed with impunity by the strong. Therefore I assumed this authority in order to protect the Moslems and combat their enemies and ensure the safety of their roads and hold my subjects in hand, until they agree and consent with one voice to the election of a man whom they approve. To him I will resign my office, and I will acknowledge his authority like any other Moslem. Take this message from me to the Moslem people! I am ready to abdicate as soon as they shall have agreed upon a chief." "Farewell," said the stranger, "God's mercy and blessings on you all!" On his departure, Ma'mún ordered 'Alí son of Ṣáliḥ to have him followed and ascertain where he was going. The chamberlain obeyed. When he returned, he said, "O Prince of the Faithful, I despatched some of my agents after him. He went to a mosque in which were fifteen men resembling him in dress and appearance. They said to him, 'Didst thou meet the man?' 'Yes,' he replied. 'What did he say to thee?' 'Nothing but good: he told me that he had taken control of affairs in order to keep the roads safe and maintain the pilgrimage and carry on the holy war and defend the oppressed and see to it that the divine laws do not become vain; but when the Moslems agree upon a chief, he will abdicate and hand over his authority to the man of their choice.' They answered that they saw no harm in that; and dispersed forthwith."

Yaḥyà added in conclusion: "Ma'mún turned to me and said, 'O Abú Muḥammad, we have satisfied these folk very easily." "O Prince of the Faithful," I replied, "glory to God, who has inspired thee with sure and right judgment in word and deed."

50

Pearl-fishing

The pearl-fishing in the Persian Ocean lasts from the beginning of Nísán (April) to the end of Ailúl (September); there is no fishing during the rest of the year. In our earlier works we have enumerated all the pearl-fisheries in this ocean, which is the only one where pearls are to be found:

they are peculiar to the sea that washes the coasts of Abyssinia and Khárak and Ḳuṭur and 'Umán and Sarandíb (Ceylon) and other countries. We have also mentioned how the pearl is formed and the different opinions attributing its origin to rain-drops and to many things besides, and have described pearls of both sorts, namely, the ancient and those of recent formation, which are called *maḥár* and known as *balbal*. The flesh and fat in the shell is an animal: it feels alarm for the pearl within it on account of the divers, as a mother fears for her child. Concerning the manner of diving, we have previously explained that the divers never touch meat, but live on fish and dates and similar foods, and how they slit their ears at the base to make an exit for the breath instead of the nostrils, because they plug the latter with something made of *dhabl*, that is, the shell of the sea-tortoise which is used for making combs, or of horn, but not of wood: it penetrates the nostrils like an iron arrow-head. In their ears they put oiled cotton, and when they are at the bottom of the sea a little of the oil exudes and gives them a bright light. They smear their feet and legs with black pigment for fear of being swallowed by the sea-beasts: the blackness scares these monsters. The divers at the bottom of the sea utter piercing cries like a dog's yelp in order to make themselves heard by one another. All this we have related in our preceding books with much curious information about the divers and the pearl-fishing, the pearl and its animal, and the qualities, marks, prices, and weights of pearls.

51

Character of the Caliph Muhtadí

Muhtadí-billah had set himself to lead a virtuous and religious life. He called the men of learning to his court, conferred dignities on the divines, and included them all in his bounty and affection. He used to say, "O sons of Háshim, let me follow the path trodden by 'Umar the son of 'Abdu 'l-'Azíz, so that I may be amongst you what 'Umar was amongst the sons of Umaiya[1]." He restricted luxury in

[1] The "sons of Háshim" are the 'Abbásids, whose ancestor, 'Abbás, was Háshim's grandson. 'Umar son of 'Abdu 'l-'Azíz, the eighth Umaiyad Caliph, was a man of great piety.

articles of dress and furniture and food and drink. By his command the gold and silver vessels in the treasury were put out and broken and coined into dinars and dirhems; and he gave orders that the painted figures adorning the rooms of the palace should be effaced. He slaughtered the rams which were set to butt against each other in the presence of the Caliphs, and the fighting-cocks, and killed all the wild beasts in the menagerie. He also forbade the use of brocade carpets and every sort of rug or carpet that is not expressly sanctioned by the Mohammedan religious law. It was the custom of the Caliphs before him to spend 10,000 dirhems daily on their table, but Muhtadí abolished that practice and assigned a sum of about 100 dirhems to meet the daily cost of his table and his entire maintenance. Often he would fast for several days at a time. It is said that after he was murdered his baggage was removed from the place where he had sought refuge, and they came upon a small padlocked chest which belonged to him. On opening it, instead of the money or jewels which it was supposed to contain, they found a *jubba* (shirt) of wool or camel's hair and an iron collar. They questioned his attendant, who declared that as soon as darkness fell, the Caliph used to put on the *jubba* and the collar and pray, bowing and prostrating himself, until dawn; and that he would sleep for an hour after the second night-prayer and then rise. Shortly before his assassination, when he had performed the prayer of sunset and was about to break his fast, one of his intimate friends heard him say, "O God, it is a true saying of Thy apostle Mohammed (God bless him!), that Thou dost never turn away the supplication of a just Imám—and I have taken pains to act justly towards my people; or of one who is wronged—and I am suffering wrong; or of one who has not yet broken his fast—and I am still fasting." Having uttered these words, he began to call down vengeance on his enemies and pray that he might be delivered from their violence.

52

A ghost story from Baghdád

In this year (A.H. 284 = A.D. 897) the Caliph Mu'taḍid saw an apparition. It appeared in his palace in various guises, now as a white-bearded anchorite wearing the customary garb of Christian ascetics; now as a handsome youth, who had a black beard and a different kind of dress; now as an old man with a white beard and in the attire of a merchant. Sometimes it held in its hand a drawn sword, with which it smote and killed the Caliph's attendants. Although the doors were shut and bolted, it used to appear wherever he was—in a room or court or any other place. He saw it on the roof of the palace which he had built for himself. There was much talk about it: the story spread amongst high and low and was carried abroad by the caravans. As to the nature of the apparition, every one had his own theory. Some thought the Caliph was haunted and tormented by a malignant demon, while others maintained that it was a believing Jinní (spirit) who, seeing him set on a course of crime and bloodshed, appeared in order to restrain and deter him. According to others, a servant in the palace had fallen in love with one of the Caliph's slave-girls, and by invoking the aid of (natural) philosophy had contrived some peculiar drugs which rendered him invisible when he put them in his mouth; but all this is conjecture and speculation. Mu'taḍid summoned the enchanters. He became exceedingly agitated and alarmed, and in his distraction he slaughtered or drowned a number of his male and female servants; others he flogged and imprisoned. In our book entitled *Akhbáru 'l-zamán* (the History of the World) we have related the whole story, together with the opinion attributed to Plato on the subject, as well as what happened to Shighb, mother of the Caliph Muḳtadir, and the reason why al-Mu'taḍid threw her into gaol and wished to disfigure her by cutting off her nose.

MUTANABBÍ

THE name of Mutanabbí (died in A.D. 965) will always be remembered in connexion with that of his patron, the Ḥamdánid prince Saifu'ddaula, whose court at Aleppo was thronged with poets and eminent literary men. Any one who reads him in Arabic must admire the splendour of his rhetoric, the luxuriance of his imagination, and the energy and aptness of his diction; but in a translation these great qualities are overshadowed by others less pleasing to our taste, which have left their mark on the poetic style of many who wrote after him in Arabic or Persian.

53

How glows mine heart for him whose heart to me is cold,
Who liketh ill my case and me in fault doth hold!
Why should I hide a love that hath worn thin my frame?
To Saifu'ddaula all the world avows the same.
Though love of his high star unites us, would that we
According to our love might so divide the fee!
Him have I visited when sword in sheath was laid,
And I have seen him when in blood swam every blade:
Him, both in peace and war the best of all mankind,
Whose crown of excellence was still his noble mind.

Do foes by flight escape thine onset, thou dost gain
A chequered victory, half of pleasure, half of pain.
So puissant is the fear thou strik'st them with, it stands
Instead of thee and works more than thy warriors' hands.
Unfought the field is thine: thou need'st not further strain
To chase them from their holes in mountain or in plain.
What! 'fore thy fierce attack whene'er an army reels,
Must thy ambitious soul press hot upon their heels?
Thy task it is to rout them on the battle-ground:
No shame to thee if they in flight have safety found.
Or thinkest thou, perchance, that victory is sweet
Only when scimitars and necks each other greet?

O justest of the just save in thy deeds to me!
Thou art accused and thou, O Sire, must judge the plea.
Look, I implore thee, well! Let not thine eye cajoled
See fat in empty froth, in all that glisters gold!
What use and profit reaps a mortal of his sight,
If darkness unto him be indistinct from light?

My deep poetic art the blind have eyes to see,
My verses ring in ears as deaf as deaf can be.
They wander far abroad whilst I am unaware,
But men collect them watchfully with toil and care.
Oft hath my laughing mien prolonged the insulter's sport
Until with claw and mouth I cut his rudeness short.
Ah, when the lion bares his teeth, suspect his guile,
Nor fancy that the lion shows to thee a smile!

I have slain the foe that sought my heart's blood, many a time,
Riding a noble mare whose back none else may climb,
Whose hind and fore-legs seem in galloping as one;
Nor hand nor foot requireth she to urge her on.
And oh, the days when I have swung my fine-edged glaive
Amidst a sea of death where wave was dashed on wave!
The desert knows me well, the night, the mounted men,
The battle and the sword, the paper and the pen!

54

Shame hitherto was wont my tears to stay,
But now by shame they will no more be stayed,
So that each bone seems through its skin to sob,
And every vein to swell the sad cascade.
Her beauty could dismay the young gazelle:
No wonder stricken me it hath dismayed.
She uncovered: pallor veiled her at farewell:
No veil 'twas, yet her cheeks it cast in shade;
So seemed they, while tears trickled over them,
Gold with a double row of pearls inlaid.
She loosed three sable tresses of her hair,
And thus of night four nights at once she made;
But when she lifted to the moon in heaven
Her face, two moons together I surveyed.

55

Naught kills the noble like forgiveness—yet
Where are the noble who no boon forget?
Kindness subdues the man of generous race,
But only makes more insolent the base.
As ill doth bounty in sword's place accord
With honour as in bounty's place the sword.

56

That which souls desire is too small a thing for them to fight about and perish by each other's hands,
Howbeit a true man will face grim Fate ere he suffer contumely.

If the life of aught that lives were lasting, we should reckon the brave the most misguided of us,
But if there is no escape from death, 'tis but weakness to be a coward.
All that the soul finds hard before it has come to pass is easy when it comes.

57

Men from their kings alone their worth derive,
But Arabs ruled by aliens cannot thrive:
Boors without culture, without noble fame,
Who know not loyalty and honour's name.
Go where thou wilt, thou seest in every land
Folk driven like cattle by a servile band.

*Rúdakí

The most famous bard of the Sámánid epoch (tenth century). He is said to have been blind from birth.

58

Rúdakí the harp will play,
'Gin ye the wine, as he the lay.
Molten ruby or ruby wine,
None who sees it may divine,
Since Nature of one stuff did shape
The solid gem, the liquid grape.
Untouched, it stains the fingers red;
Untasted, flies into the head.

*Abú Zurá'a of Jurján

A court minstrel, who flourished under the Sámánids.

59

When silver they ask of me, gold I fling;
The power of my song, when they bid me sing,
Makes wax of stubborn steel.
When the wind's abroad, with the wind I roam:
Now with cup and lute I leave my home,
Now armed from head to heel.

*Daḳíḳí

Died in A.D. 975. He began the *Sháhnáma*, the Persian national epic, which was completed by Firdausí.

60

O would that in the world there were no night,
That I might ne'er be parted from her lips!
No scorpion-sting would sink deep in my heart
But for her scorpion coils of darkest hair.
If 'neath her lip no starry dimple shone,
I would not linger with the stars till day;
And if she were not cast in beauty's mould,
My soul would not be moulded of her love.
If I must live without my Well-belov'd,
O God! I would there were no life for me.

*Kisá'í of Merv

Died about A.D. 990.

61

Unclose thine eyes and deeply gaze on the saffron-flower[1]
Shining amidst the grass-blades, a very pearl in sheen,
Even as a shamefaced lover, to hide his blushing cheeks,
Draws to his face the mantle in folds of satin green.

The wine thro' darting sunbeams how sweet and fair to see!
But oh, when falls reflected therein the radiant shower,
The blue glass and red vintage and golden-yellow rays
Are violet, you'ld fancy, and poppy and saffron-flower.

So bright 'tis, when it trickles down from the goblet's mouth,
You'ld say from pearls is trickling cornelian red and fine;
So clear 'tis, when you pour it in the hollow of your palm,
Nor palm from cup you ever would know, nor cup from wine.

[1] Meadow saffron or crocus.

62

Roses are a gift of price
Sent to us from Paradise;
More divine our nature grows
In the Eden of the rose.

Roses why for silver sell?
O rose-merchant, fairly tell
What you buy instead of those
That is costlier than the rose.

*Firdausí

The charming tale of which the best part is translated in the following pages may have been composed by Firdausí in his youth and afterwards inserted by him in the *Sháhnáma*; for it has metrical peculiarities which distinguish it from the rest of the poem. Here Firdausí shows himself as great a master of the romantic style as elsewhere of the epic.

63

The Tale of Bízhan and Manízha[1]

I

He donned a glistening robe of Rúm
And stuck in his tiar an eagle's plume.
They saddled Shabrang, and he bade them bring
His baldrick and knightly signet-ring,
And leaped to the stirrup and drew not rein:
Thither he rode with might and main.
Deep thoughts of love his heart beguiled
As he neared that forest wild.
How yearningly his way he bent
Anigh the fair Manízha's tent,
And from the sun took shelter free
Beneath a lofty cypress tree!
The mead rang loud with harp and song,
As though to cheer his soul along.

[1] Manízha was the daughter of Afrásiyáb, the King of Túrán, while her lover, Bízhan son of Gív, was an Iranian knight. The reader will recollect that Írán and Túrán in the *Sháhnáma* correspond to Greece and Troy in the *Iliad*.

Whenas the beauty in her bower
Espied the warrior paladin,
Whose cheeks star-bright were like the flower
Of violet and jessamine,
His breast aglow with Greek brocade,
His head crowned with a golden tiar,
Love swelled the bosom of the maid
For him who burned in love-desire;
And to her nurse she said, "Be thou
My messenger. 'Neath yonder tree
Who is that handsome youth? Go now,
I pray thee, nurse, go quick and see!
Is he Siyáwush come anew
To life, or child of elfin race?
And ask how he came here, and who
Hath ever brought him to this place?
Say, 'Art thou man or sprite, that thus
With raging fire of love for thee
Thou kindlest all the hearts of us?—
The world's Doomsday it well might be.
For in this meadow each springtide
Have I kept holiday, and ne'er
Year in, year out, have we espied
Any but thee, O tall and fair!
But whether man or elf benign
Upon our greenwood feast thou stray,
I never looked on face like thine:
What is thy name, and whence thy way?'"

To Bízhan came the nurse and bowed
With homage low and blessing loud.
She told him all Manízha said,
His two cheeks bloomed like roses red.
"Sweet messenger, I am not the knight
Siyáwush, nor am I a sprite
Of faery pedigree;
(Thus Bízhan joyously began)
Hither I come from old Iran,
The country of the free.

Bízhan, the son of Gív, my name:
Full keen to fight the boar I came,
The cloven heads by the wayside fling,
And bear their tushes to the King;
But when I heard of revels here,
I sped not back: the hope lay near,
Afrásiyáb's daughter I may trace
And win, by happy fortune's grace,
If but in dream to see her face.
Now richly dight are the meadows green,
Gay as an idol-house in Chín.
I'll give for thy good rede and care
Gold crown, a girdle, earrings fine,
If thou wilt lead me to the fair
And move her heart to love as mine."

The nurse returned and whispered clear
The secret in Manízha's ear,
Described his look and every limb
Even as the Maker fashioned him.
Manízha sent this answer straight:
"What was thy fancy is thy prize,
Come to me with a lover's gait
And fill with light my soul and eyes!
At sight of thee will roses reign
O'er sunken vale and tented plain."
He heard, and recked of naught beside,
The messenger became the guide.

Forth from the cypress shade in haste—
For parley 'twas no hour—
He footed. Belt of gold was laced
About his cypress-slender waist
As entered he the bower.
Manízha clasped him to her breast,
Undid the royal zone, and pressed
To hear of road and toil and war:
"Who came with thee to fight the boar?
And why, with such a form and face,
Why troublest thou to wield the mace?"

With musk and rose-water his feet
They laved, then hasted to set meat.
Viands of every sort they spread
In plenty more and more, and redd
A paradise of wine and song
And cleared the tent of all its throng,
Save handmaidens to wait on foot
And music make with harp and lute.
Brocade of peacock's hue and pied
With dinars like a leopard's hide
Upon the floor was strewn;
With ambergris and musk blown wide
And gold and gems from side to side
The gay pavilion shone.
Three days, three nights in pleasure passed,
Old wine in crystal cups went round,
Till Bízhan, overcome at last,
Slept where he lay in drunken swound.

II

Manízha, when the time drew nigh
For parting, fain would rest her eye
On Bízhan. When she saw him sad,
She called her handmaidens and bade
Them mingle in the wine's sweet draught
A drug that steals the sense. By craft
They gave it him, and as he drank,
His head inebriated sank.
Straight she prepared a palanquin,
The sleeping youth was laid within.
On one side was a pleasure-seat,
A couch on the other, all complete
Of sandal-wood. She sprinkled there
Camphor and shed the rose-water.
Soon as they neared Turania's town
She wrapped him in a hooded gown,
And entered secretly at night
The palace—none but friends knew how—
Made ready a chamber of delight,

And eager for his waking now,
Poured in his ear a medicine
That quickly the dulled sense uncharms:
He woke and found the jessamine
Sweet-bosomed lady in his arms.
Afrásiyáb's palace! In duress,
And bowered with the fair princess

Bízhan in bitter rue implored:
"Save me from Ahriman, O Lord!
For me, alas, 'tis all too clear,
Never will be escape from here.
But oh, avenge me on Gurgín!
Oh, hearken to my curses fell!
'Twas he that lured me to this teen,
Enchanting me with many a spell."
"Be of brave cheer," Manízha cried,
"What is not come deem wind and vain;
To men all sorts of things betide,
The feast anon, the fight again."

Betwixt the spousal and the doom
These lovers 'gan array a room
For banqueting and glee.
From each alcove tripped into sight
The damsels beautiful and bright
As rose-cheeked fays, and all bedight
With Chinese taffety,
Who played the harp and trilled the lay
And sped the fleeting night and day.
So passed a while. The doorkeeper
Got news that mischief was astir,
But since a rash word raised on bruit
Shakes down from sorrow's tree the fruit,
He searched the maze to find a track,
Looked deeply in and cast far back—
"Who is he? Of what race? What plan
Or hope hath led him to Turan?"—
And so discovered all, and pale
For his own life if he should fail

To speak out, from his post took wing
And went before Turania's king,
And said, "Thy daughter hath a man,
A lover chosen from Iran."
The monarch cried to God, his form
Trembled as willow in the storm;
Then from his eyelashes he strook
The tears of blood and raging spoke:
"Whoso in bower doth daughter hold,
Ill-starred is he, tho' crowned with gold."

III

Afrásiyáb bade Garsíwaz there
Dark dungeon, heavy chains, prepare.
"Go chain his hands to Roman gyve
Arched like a bridge; and see thou drive
The massive bolts right in: each limb
Make fast from head to foot of him;
Then cast him headlong in the pit
That ne'er by sun or moon is lit.
Take elephants, get hither drawn
The boulder of the fiend Akwán,
Which plucked from ocean deeps was hurled
Upon the borders of the world
Amidst a wood of Chín, to block
The pit Arzhang. Let that huge rock
Seal Bízhan's prison till he deranged
With anguish be, and I revenged!
Thence to Manízha fly apace,
The wanton who hath shamed her race.
Go with thy knights and sack her hall,
Strip her of wealth and crown and all!
Say, 'O accursed and reviled,
Unworthy of the throne and tiar,
Thou hast the diadem defiled,
Brought low the proud head of thy sire.'
Ay, drag her naked to the abyss,
And bid her on her prince look well
And share his tears, whom he would kiss,
And do him service in his cell.

Better to fight and die with fame
Than live to see this day of shame."
The monarch's ruthless will upon
Bízhan, the son of Gív, was done.
They haled him from the gallows, bound,
And bore him to the pit, and round
His waist a Roman gyve they cast,
Whereto his hands they fettered fast,
While smiths with steel hammers swung free
Drave deep the heavy bolts. So he
Headlong into the pit was thrown,
And o'er its mouth they set the stone.
Thence to Manízha's palace spurred
Garsíwaz and his cavaliers.
Whenas of them the princess heard,
Her face was hidden by her tears.
He gave her treasuries to loot,
Purses and crowns bestowed and bore;
Left her bare-headed and bare-foot
And with a single wrap, no more.
He sped her to the pit: her eyes
Shed blood, her cheeks were fresh as spring.
"Here is thy house and home," he cries,
"Wait on this bondsman of the king!"
When fierce Garsíwaz rode away,
Manízha was to sorrow wed,
Far o'er the desert she did stray
Until a day and night had fled;
Then, sobbing loud, came nigh the prison
And made a passage for one hand;
And ever when the sun was risen,
The livelong day she roamed the land
And gathered food and let it down
To Bízhan through the crevice small,
Weeping the while with many a moan:
Thus wretchedly she lived in thrall.

IV

By looking into a magic cup, Kai Khusrau, the Sháh of Írán, discovers what has befallen Bízhan and sends Rustam, disguised as a merchant, to rescue him from captivity.

At tidings of the caravan,
Bare-headed to the city ran
Manízha, weeping sore.
To Rustam flew the fair princess,
And wiping from her eyelashes
With sleeve the tears, 'gan hail and bless
And piteously implore.
"Hast joy of health and wealth?" said she;
"Thy labour mayst thou never rue!
High Heaven grant thy wish to thee,
No evil eye a mischief do!
With heart of hope sith thou hast tied
Thy girdle, may thy gain increase!
May wisdom ever be thy guide,
Iran live happy and at peace!
What news of the Sháh's knights hast thou—
Gív, Gúdarz, and the Iranian arms?
Of Bízhan hear they not by now?
Bring they no aid against his harms?
Will they not come, his noble sires,
To save the youth of Gúdarz' race?
Will they not break the iron tires
That hold him in a fell embrace?
His feet in heavy chains are wound,
His hands with the smiths' rivets sore.
Poor soul! in fetters dragged, fast-bound,
And all his raiment stained with gore!
For me, I roam in restless fears,
His wailings fill mine eyes with tears."

Bold Rustam at her words took fright,
Fain would he chase her from his sight.
"Begone!" he bawled, "thou speak'st in vain
Of Khusrau and the youthful thane.

Nor Gív nor Gúdarz do I know,
Thy chatter hath made me foolish. Go!"
Manízha looked on him and dewed
Her bosom with tears that gushed in streams.
She said, "O master wise and good,
Not thee such ruthless speech beseems.
Tell naught, but chase me not from thee,
For oh, with pain my heart is torn.
'Tis custom in Iran, maybe,
To give no news to them that mourn."
"What ails thee, woman?" Rustam said,
"Sure, Ahriman hath turned thy head.
My trafficking thou mad'st me leave,
Therefore I scolded thee. But grieve
No more for words of hasty fret:
My thoughts upon my trade were set.
And further, thou must understand
I dwell not in Kai Khusrau's land.
Gúdarz and Gív I know not: in
Those marches I have never been."
What food was there he bade them lay
Before the beggar-maid straightway;
Then questions, one by one, put he,
As "Why is fortune dark with thee?
Iran why ask of, and why scan
The road that leadeth to Iran?"

"What need to ask me how I fare,
Of all my woe and all my care?
From yon pit's mouth, O noble man,
Grief-laden unto thee I ran,
To ask of thee the news I crave
Of Gúdarz and of Gív the brave;
And thou at me didst warlike bawl—
Ah, fear'st thou not the Judge of all?
Afrásiyáb's daughter, I am she,
Manízha! Ne'er the sun might see
Me bare who now with bloodshot eyes
And teenful heart and cheeks how wan,
Gathering bread in beggar's guise,
From door to door must wander on.

This is God's doom on me. I fell
For Bízhan's sake from tiar and throne.
Can fortune be more miserable
Than this? God end it for me soon!
And Bízhan in the pit profound
Nor sun nor moon nor night nor day
Beholds, where riveted and bound
He prayeth God for death alway.
Hence griefs on griefs still o'er me rise,
Hence flow these waters from mine eyes.
Now, if thy way Iran-ward turn,
Of Gúdarz haply thou wilt learn,
Or peradventure Gív behold
At Khusrau's gate, or Rustam bold.
Say, 'Bízhan is in dungeon fast,
And if thou lag, his day is past.
Wouldst thou him see, to horse, to heel!
Above him stone, below him steel.'"
Rustam replied, "These tears of love
Why rainest thou? Nay, why not move
Thy noble well-wishers to sue,
Lady, for thee before thy sire?
Perchance he will pity thee: anew
His blood may stir, his heart take fire.
Had not I stood of him in fear,
I would have given thee countless gear."
Then to the cooks: "Go, bring with speed
Viands according to her need."
A fowl hot from the spit fetched they,
He wrapped it in soft bread himself,
And hid therein his ring away
With hand as nimble as an elf.
"This to the dungeon take, O guide
Of them that have no help beside!"

V

Back to the pit's mouth sped in haste
Manízha, clasping to her breast
The viands in a kerchief wound
And gave to Bízhan all. Astound

He gazed, and forth from the abyss
Called to the sun-cheeked damozel,
"Whence, O belovèd, gott'st thou this,
That thy return is sped so well?
What toil and hardship hast thou borne,
Kind heart, to succour me forlorn!"
Manízha said, "A caravan
Is come with goodly merchandise.
'Tis a rich trader from Iran,
With jewels, every sort and size—
A noble, wise, and glorious man,
A man of wealth and open heart;
Before his house he holds a mart—
He gave me this and bade me pray
To God for him, and said, 'Away!
Go to the prisoner in his den.
If more he need, come thou again.'"

Bízhan amidst his fears grew bold
With hope as he the bread unrolled.
He ate, and turning from his meal
Espied the hidden ring. The seal
He looked on, read the name, intent,
And laughed in joy and wonderment.
A turquoise seal it was, and there
Stood "Rustam" graven fine as hair!
He saw the pledge of friendship true,
The key of sorrow's lock he knew,
And laughed with such a royal shout,
The rising echoes rang without.
Manízha, when she heard the peal
From dungeon dark and chains of steel,
Marvelled and uttered this sooth rede:
"The mad will laugh at their own deed."
Then spoke, amazed, the princess mild,
"Good youth, what means this laughter wild?
How ope thy lips to laugh, when light
To thee is dark and day is night?
Tell all, with me the secret share!
Hath Fortune shown a face more fair?"

Her answered Bízhan, "Hope have I
This hard coil Fortune will untie.
Now, if with me thou wilt keep troth
And make a covenant on oath,
I'll tell thee all. A woman's tongue,
Tho' sewed her lips, will out ere long."
Manízha bitterly did moan:
"What curse is fallen on me?" she cries.
"Alas, for I am left alone
With bleeding heart and weeping eyes.
Doth Bízhan think of me so ill,
Who gave my heart and home and all,
To run in rags o'er plain and hill,
An outcast from my father's hall?
I gave to plunder gems and tiars
And wealth and treasure, all for him.
He was my hope: my hope expires,
My world is dark, mine eyes are dim.
His secret he would hide from me!
Thou know'st me better, Lord, than he."
"'Tis true," said Bízhan. "For my sake
Thou hast lost every thing but life.
Now must I tell and counsel take
With thee, my wise and loving wife.
Rede me in all, 'tis meet and fit:
My woe hath emptied me of wit.
Know that this jewel-merchant man
Whose cook to thee gave the sweet food,
'Tis my cause brings him to Turan,
Else jewels were to him no good.
God hath had ruth on me. Maybe,
The earth's broad face I yet shall see.
Me will this man from long-drawn bane,
Thee from hot haste and melting pain
Deliver. Go, say in his ear,
'O Persia's kingly cavalier,
Soft heart to help, strong arm to guide,
Dost thou on Rakhsh to battle ride?'"

Fleet as the wind, Manízha sped
To Rustam, and the message said;

Who, when he heard the damsel speak
That far had come his aid to seek,
Knew Bízhan had laid the secret bare
To the rose-cheeked lady cypress-fair.
"O beauteous countenance!" cried he,
"May God ne'er part thy love and thee!
Say, 'Yes: the Power that heard in heaven
Thy call for aid, to thee hath given
The lord of Rakhsh. A weary road
From Zábul to Iran he trod
For thee, and thence came travel-worn
To Túr. Ah, wretched as thou art,
What sorrow must thou not have borne
This many a day within thine heart!'
Go tell him this and secret keep,
Listen at night for my proclaim,
Cull faggots in the forest deep,
At nightfall rouse a beacon-flame!"

Manízha, blithe and freed from care,
Ran to the mountain-dungeon where
Her woeful lover lay.
"I gave the message," she began,
"To that renowned and blessed man,
And this he bade me say:
'Yea, I am he, 'tis sooth I speak,
Whose name the son of Gív doth seek.
O thou that runn'st with heart-wound sore,
Thy fair cheeks bathed in tears and gore,
Tell him my loins and hands are scarred
For his sake as a spotted pard.
Now, since of him we sure are made,
Soon shall he see my killing blade;
Now in my grasp rent earth shall groan,
And high be hurled that sunken stone.'
He bade me, when the sky grows dun
And night slips from the leash of sun,
Kindle a beacon-fire, that night
Round the pit's head may be as bright

As day. 'I by its blaze (he said)
Will find the way and boldly tread.'"

When Bízhan deep in murky den
This message heard, he joyed, and then
To God he lifted up his face:
"O holy Giver of all grace
Who succourest me in every woe,
O God, pierce to the heart my foe!
Right me on him that did the wrong,
Thou know'st my grief and pain how long.
Again may I my country find
And leave this baleful star behind!
But thou who gavest, O my bride,
For me thy body and soul and heart,
Who, by such bitter sorrow tried,
Thought'st all a joy that eased my smart;
Lett'st girdle, throne, and tiar go
And kindred's love and parent's ruth—
If from this Dragon's claws I know
Deliverance in my time of youth,
Oh, like a godly worshipper
I'll run to thee with arms flung wide,
And gird my loins to make thee fair
Return, as slaves a king beside.
Bear now this further toil: 'twill bring
Thee wealth and many a precious thing."

Manízha flitted at his word
Into the forest like a bird.
She filled her arms with wood, her eyes
Still watched the sun for night to rise.
Whenas the sun was seen no more
And dark night marched the mountains o'er,
What hour the world takes rest entire
And all is dim where all was bright,
Manízha set ablaze a fire
That scorched the eye of pitchy night,
While sounded in her ear the drum
Which told that brass-hoofed Rakhsh was come.

RUSTAM ABOUT TO RESCUE BÍZHAN FROM THE PIT INTO WHICH HE WAS CAST BY AFRÁSIYÁB

*'Unṣurí

Laureate of Sultan Maḥmúd of Ghazna. He died about the middle of the eleventh century.

64

A scene like Paradise! 'Tis not Farkhár[1],
Yet all the splendour of Farkhár is there.
Kisses of loyal kings imprint the earth,
Faces of fair youths fill with light the air.
Then look how gold and silver Pleiades
Bestud the rolling sky of scimitars,
And how, like dagger's pearl-encrusted haft,
Each baldrick shows its blazonry of stars!
Mark yonder troop belted with golden swords,
Whereon pomegranate-red you may behold
Rubies like tears of blood distilled in pain
From lover's eyes o'er cheeks as pale as gold.
On the ranked elephants their golden harness
Glitters like saffron flowers on some hillside;
Serpents their trunks might seem: in such a coat
Of golden scales the serpent's self doth glide.
Darkful as thunderclouds, with dagger-tusks,
Their mountain-forms move wind-like o'er the plain.
What place is this? The battle-field, in sooth,
Of the world's Emperor and Suzerain!

*Masrúr ibn Muḥammad of Ṭálaḳán

The following passage occurs in a panegyric addressed to Aḥmad ibn Ḥasan al-Maimandí, the Vizier of Sultan Maḥmúd.

65

When from the night's dark rising a little space had past,
That beauty springlike-joyous into the garden came—
Her loveliness so tender, peris would worship it;
Before her jewelled splendour idols would kiss the earth.
The treasurer of Glory she robbed of his guarded grace,
From the fair maids of Khoten she bore the palm away—
And whispering softly, softly, spake to me: "Why," said she,

[1] A city in Turkistán, famous for the beauty of its inhabitants.

"Why art thou fain to leave me? What is this purpose fell?
Ah, stay, for here beside me spring reigns in autumn's stead;
My cheeks are damask roses, my chin a white lily.
And rest thine eye on the wine-cup, then wilt thou praise no more
The tulip's rain-washed petals, the dew-bright jessamine."

*ABÚ SA'ÍD IBN ABI 'L-KHAIR

THE great Persian mystic (A.D. 967–1049), to whom many quatrains are attributed. See Professor Browne's *Literary History of Persia*, vol. II, pp. 261–269 and my *Studies in Islamic Mysticism*, pp. 1–76.

66

He was asked, "When shall a man be freed from his wants?" "When God shall free him," he replied; "this is not effected by a man's exertion, but by the grace and help of God. First of all, He brings forth in him the desire to attain this goal. Then He opens to him the gate of repentance. Then He throws him into self-mortification, so that he continues to strive and, for a while, to pride himself upon his efforts, thinking that he is advancing or achieving something; but afterwards he falls into despair and feels no joy. Then he knows that his work is not pure, but tainted, he repents of the acts of devotion which he had thought to be his own, and perceives that they were done by God's grace and help, and that he was guilty of polytheism in attributing them to his own exertion. When this becomes manifest, a feeling of joy enters his heart. Then God opens to him the gate of certainty, so that for a time he takes anything from any one and accepts contumely and endures abasement, and knows for certain by Whom it is brought to pass, and doubt concerning this is removed from his heart. Then God opens to him the gate of love, and here too egoism shows itself for a time and he is exposed to blame, which means that in his love of God he meets fearlessly whatever may befall him and recks not of reproach; but still he thinks 'I love' and finds no rest until he perceives that it is God who loves him and keeps him in the state of loving, and that this is the result of divine love and grace, not of his own endeavour. Then

God opens to him the gate of unity and causes him to know that all action depends on God Almighty. Hereupon he perceives that all is He, and all is by Him, and all is His; that He has laid this self-conceit upon His creatures in order to prove them, and that He in His omnipotence ordains that they shall hold this false belief, because omnipotence is His attribute, so that when they regard His attributes they shall know that He is the Lord. What formerly was hearsay now becomes known to him intuitively as he contemplates the works of God. Then he entirely recognises that he has not the right to say 'I' or 'mine.' At this stage he beholds his helplessness; desires fall away from him and he becomes free and calm. He wishes that which God wishes; his own wishes are gone, he is emancipated from his wants, and has gained peace and joy in both worlds....First, action is necessary, then knowledge, in order that thou mayst know that thou knowest naught and art no one. This is not easy to know. It is a thing that cannot be rightly learned by instruction, nor sewed on with needle nor tied on with thread. It is the gift of God."

67

The heart's vision is what matters, not the tongue's speech. Thou wilt never escape from thy self until thou slay it. To say "There is no god but Allah" is not enough. Most of those who make the verbal profession of faith are polytheists at heart, and polytheism is the one unpardonable sin. Thy whole body is full of doubt and polytheism. Thou must cast them out in order to be at peace. Until thou deny thy self thou wilt never believe in God. Thy self, which is keeping thee far from God and saying, "So-and-so has treated thee ill," "such and such a one has done well by thee," points the way to creatureliness; and all this is polytheism. Nothing depends on the creatures, all depends on the Creator. This thou must know and say, and having said it thou must stand firm. To stand firm means that when thou hast said "One," thou must never again say "Two." Creator *and* creature are "Two."...Do not double like a fox, that ye may suddenly start up in some other place: that is not right faith. Say "Allah!" and stand firm there. Standing firm is this, that when thou hast said "God" thou shouldst no more speak or think of created things, so that it is just as though they were not....Love that One who does not cease to be when thou ceasest, in order that thou mayst be such a being that thou never wilt cease to be!

68

Four thousand years before God created these bodies, He created the souls and kept them beside Himself and shed a light upon them. He knew what quantity of light each soul received and He was showing favour to each in proportion to its illumination. The souls remained all that time in the light until they became fully nourished. Those who in this world live in joy and agreement with one another must have been akin to one another in yonder place. Here they love one another and are called the friends of God, and they are brethren who love one another for God's sake. These souls know each other by the smell, like horses. Though one be in the East and the other in the West, yet they feel joy and comfort in each other's talk, and one who lives in a later generation than the other is instructed and consoled by the words of his friend.

69

O Thou in whose bat well-curved my heart like a ball is laid,
Nor ever a hairbreadth swerved from Thy bidding nor disobeyed,
I have washed mine outward clean, the water I drew and poured;
Mine inward is Thy demesne—do Thou keep it stainless, Lord!

70

In my heart Thou dwellest—else with blood I'll drench it;
In mine eye Thou glowest—else with tears I'll quench it.
Only to be one with Thee my soul desireth,
Else from out my body, by hook or crook, I'll wrench it!

71

Cheer one sad heart: thy loving deed will be
More than a thousand temples raised by thee.
One freeman whom thy kindness hath enslaved
Outweighs by far a thousand slaves set free.

72

Not until every mosque beneath the sun
Lies ruined, will our holy work be done;
And never will true Musalmán appear
Till faith and infidelity are one.

*BÁBÁ KÚHÍ OF SHÍRÁZ

DIED in A.D. 050. He was a dervish contemporary with Abú Sa'íd ibn Abi 'l-Khair, and his *Díwán*, preserved in the British Museum, is the oldest collection of mystical odes in Persian that has come down to us.

73

In the market, in the cloister—only God I saw.
In the valley and on the mountain—only God I saw.
Him I have seen beside me oft in tribulation;
In favour and in fortune—only God I saw.
In prayer and fasting, in praise and contemplation,
In the religion of the Prophet—only God I saw.
Neither soul nor body, accident nor substance,
Qualities nor causes—only God I saw.
I oped mine eyes and by the light of His face around me
In all the eye discovered—only God I saw.
Like a candle I was melting in his fire:
Amidst the flames outflashing—only God I saw.
Myself with mine own eyes I saw most clearly,
But when I looked with God's eyes—only God I saw.
I passed away into nothingness, I vanished,
And lo, I was the All-living—only God I saw.

Abu 'l-'Alá al-Ma'arrí

Abu 'l-'Alá, the famous pessimist, ascetic, and freethinker, was born at Ma'arra near Aleppo in A.D. 973. An early attack of smallpox left him almost blind; but his extraordinary powers of memory compensated him for the loss of his sight and enabled him to acquire a great reputation, not only as a philologist but as a man of letters and general culture. His visit to Baghdád (A.D. 1008–9) marks the turning-point in his life. The hopes which drew him thither soon faded, and he came back to his native town, where the last fifty years of his long life were spent in seclusion. During this period he composed, besides a large number of prose writings, the work which has made him better known in Europe than any other Arabic poet—the *Luzúmu má lá yalzam*. These poems both in form and matter bear the stamp of a singular personality. The author dare not always say what he means, but he says enough to show that in his view not authority and tradition, but reason and conscience, must decide whether actions are right or wrong, and whether beliefs are false or true. He applies a rationalistic standard to all revealed religions, not excepting Islam. Those who desire further information may refer to an essay entitled "The Meditations of Ma'arrí" in my *Studies in Islamic Poetry*, pp. 43–207, from which the following versions have been selected.

74

(Metre: *Ṭawíl*, with variations.)

Would that a lad had died in the very hour of birth
And never sucked, as she lay in childbed, his mother's breast!
Her babe, it says to her or ever its tongue can speak,
"Nothing thou gett'st of me but sorrow and bitter pain."

75

(Metre: *Ṭawíl*, with variations.)

'Tis God's will a man should live in torment and tribulation,
Until those that know him cry, "He hath paid now the lifelong debt."
Give joy to his next of kin on the day of his departure,
For they gain a heritage of riches, and he of peace.

76

Perish this world! I should not joy to be
Its Caliph or Maḥmúd[1].
My fate I know not, save that I in turn
Am treading the same path to the same bourne
As old 'Ád and Thamúd[2].
The mountains ('tis averred) shall melt, the seas
Surely shall freeze;
And the great dome of Heaven, whose poles
Have ever awed men's souls,
Some argue for its ruin, some maintain
Its immortality—in vain?
The scattered boulders of the lava waste,
Shall e'er they mingle into one massed ore?
If sheer catastrophe shall fling in haste
The Pleiad luminaries asunder,
Well may be quenched the fiery brand of Mars;
And if decay smites Indian scimitars,
Survival of their sheaths would be a wonder[3]!

77

In the casket of the Hours
Events deep-hid
Wait on their guardian Powers
To raise the lid.

And the Maker infinite,
Whose poem is Time,
He need not weave in it
A forced stale rhyme.

The Nights pass so,
Voices dumb,
Without sense quick or slow
Of what shall come.

* * *

[1] Sultan Maḥmúd of Ghazna died in A.D. 1030, twenty-eight years before the death of Ma'arrí.

[2] Extinct aboriginal tribes: the legend of their destruction is told in the Koran.

[3] The "scimitars" represent the stars and planets which are "sheathed" by the celestial spheres.

By Allah's will preserving
From misflight,
The barbs of Time unswerving
On us alight.

A loan is all he gives
And takes again;
With his gift happy lives
The folly of men.

78

(Metre: *Wáfir.*)

Aweary am I of living in town and village—
And oh, to be camped alone in a desert region,
Revived by the scent of lavender when I hunger
And scooping into my palm, if I thirst, well-water!
Meseemeth, the Days are dromedaries lean and jaded
That bear on their backs humanity travelling onward;
They shrink not in dread from any portentous nightmare,
Nor quail at the noise of shouting and rush of panic,
But journey along for ever with those they carry,
Until at the last they kneel by the dug-out houses.
No need, when in earth the maid rests covered over,
No need for her locks of hair to be loosed and plaited;
The young man parts from her, and his tears are flowing—
Even thus do the favours flow of disgustful Fortune.

79

They robed the Christian's daughter,
From high embowered room
In dusky robe they brought her
Down, down into a tomb—
And oh, her dress had often been
Gay as a peacock's plume.

80

(Metre: *Ṭawíl.*)

The sage looketh in the glass of Reason, but he that makes
His brethren his looking-glass will see truth, mayhap, or lies.
And I, shall I fear the pain of Allah, when He is just,

And though I have lived the life of one wronged and racked
with pain?
Yes: each hath his portioned lot; but men in their ignorance
Would mend here the things they loathe that never can
mended be.

81

Life seems the vision of one sleeping
Which contraries interpret after:
'Tis joy whenever thou art weeping,
Thy smiles are tears, and sobs thy laughter;
And Man, exulting in his breath,
A prisoner kept in chains for death.

82

(Metre: *Ṭawíl.*)

Shall ever the dead man's soul return after he is gone,
To render his kin the meed of thanks for their flowing tears?
The hearse-bearers' necks and hands conveyed him—a change
of state
From when to and fro he fared in palanquins all of gold;
And liefer had he alive been trodden below their feet
Than high they had lifted up his corpse on their shoulders
borne.
O levelling Death! to thee a rich man is like a poor,
Thou car'st not that one hath hit the right way, another missed.
The knight's coat of mail thou deem'st in softness a maiden's
shift,
And frail as the spider's house the domed halls of Chosroes.
To earth came he down unhorsed when Death in the saddle
sate,
Tho' aye 'mongst his clan was he the noblest of them that ride.
A bier is but like a ship: it casteth its wrecked away
To drown in a sea of death where wave ever mounts on wave.

83

The holy fights by Moslem heroes fought,
The saintly works by Christian hermits wrought
And those of Jewry or of Sabian creed—
Their valour reaches not the Indian's deed

Whom zeal and awe religiously inspire
To cast his body on the flaming pyre.
Yet is man's death a long, long sleep of lead
And all his life a waking. O'er our dead
The prayers are chanted, hopeless farewells ta'en;
And there we lie, never to stir again.
Shall I so fear in mother earth to rest?
How soft a cradle is thy mother's breast!
When once the viewless spirit from me is gone,
By rains unfreshened let my bones rot on!

84

(Metre: *Ṭawíl.*)

He gave to himself the name of Joy—fool and liar he!
May earth stop his mouth! In Time is anything joyful?
Yes: one part of good is there in many a thousand parts,
And when we have found it, those that follow are evil.
Our riches and poverty, precaution and heedlessness,
And glory and shame—'tis all a cheat and illusion.
Encompassed are we by Space, which cannot remove from us,
And Time, which doth ever pass away with his people.
So charge, as thou wilt, the foe, or skulk on the battle-field:
The Nights charge at thee and wheel again to the onset.

85

Ah, let us go, whom nature joined of old in friendship fast,
To meet the Fates pursuing us, that we may die at last.
The draught of Life, to me it seems the bitterest thing to drain,
And lo, in bitter sooth we all must spew it out again.

86

(Metre: *Ṭawíl.*)

Who knows? Some that fill the mosque with terror whene'er they preach
No better may be than some that drink to a tavern-tune.
If God's public worship serve them only to engine fraud,
Then nearer to Him are those forsaking it purposely.

Let none vaunt himself who soon returns to an element
Of clay which the potter takes and cunningly moulds for use.
A vessel, if so it hap, anon will be made of him,
From whence any common churl at pleasure may eat and drink;
And he, unaware the while, transported from land to land—
O sorrow for him! his bones have crumbled, he wanders on.

87

The world's abounding filth is shot
O'er all its creatures, all its kinds;
The evil taint even she hath got
Whose loom for her a living finds.
Be just and live on earth what can?
And none is more unjust than Man.

88

(Metre: *Ṭawíl.*)

To neighbour with men meseems a sickness perpetual;
I wished, when it wore me thin, for fever that comes and goes.
By effort and self-constraint they compassed a little good;
Whatever they wrought of ill, 'twas nature that prompted it.
Oh, where are the gushing streams and oceans of bounty now?
Are those of the lion's brood that Time spared hyenas all?
Their wood in the burning yields a perfume of frankincense,
But tried on the teeth of sore necessity, proves flint-hard.

89

Thou art diseased in understanding and religion. Come to me, that thou mayst hear the tidings of sound truth.
Do not unjustly eat what the water has given up, and do not desire as food the flesh of slaughtered animals,
Or the white (milk) of mothers who intended its pure draught for their young, not for noble ladies.
And do not grieve the unsuspecting birds by taking their eggs; for injustice is the worst of crimes.
And spare the honey which the bees get betimes by their industry from the flowers of fragrant plants;

For they did not store it that it might belong to others, nor did they gather it for bounty and gifts.
I washed my hands of all this; and would that I had perceived my way ere my temples grew hoar!

90

Think about things! Thought clears away some part of ignorance. Were skilled
The nesting bird to see the end, it ne'er would have begun to build.
The Indians, who cremate their dead and never visit them again,
Win peace from straitness of the grave and ordeal by the angels twain[1].
To male and female in the world the path of right is preached in vain.

91

(Metre: *Ṭawíl.*)

What! seest thou not that vice in man's nature is inborn,
But virtue a new unheired possession which minds acquire?
My heart hath been wrung to watch some morning a savage boor
Belabouring his ass with blows—he takes on his head a sin.
The tired beast beyond its strength he burdens, and if it flag,
He sets on it with his lash, whilst stubbornly it endures—
Until it grows like unto a whoremonger, one unwed,
On whom falls the penalty of scourging, and not by halves[2].
Weals rise on its back and flanks, the visible marks of woe;
Oh, pardon a helpless brute too feeble to plod along!
A Maker have we: the mind, undoubting, confesses Him
Eternal—then what avails this birth of a latter day?

[1] According to orthodox belief, when the dead man is laid in the grave he is examined by two angels, named Munkar and Nakír; hence Mohammedans take care to have their graves made hollow, that they may sit up with more ease during the inquisition.

[2] An unmarried man who commits adultery is punished by the infliction of one hundred stripes, if he be free; but if he be a slave, the number of stripes is reduced by half.

And grant that you rub and rub the fire-stick of Right in vain,
Still less from those sticks of Wrong can ever you coax a spark.
It gladdens me not, that I inflict on a fellow-man
Injustice, and live in ease and opulence all the while.

92

Allah disposes. Be a hermit, then,
And mix not with the divers sorts of men.
I know but this, that him I hold in error
Who helps to propagate Time's woe and terror.

93

Humanity, in whom the best
Of this world's features are expressed—
The chiefs set over them to reign
Are but as moons that wax and wane.

If ye unto your sons would prove
By act how dearly them ye love,
Then every voice of wisdom joins
To bid you leave them in your loins.

94

I swear, my body will cease not ever to be in pain,
Until it come to its element eterne again;
And thither when I go back, my bones that once were strong
To earth will crumble during endless ages long.

95

Metre: (*Ṭawīl.*)

And men see the last of me the day when shall o'er me close
The deep well of Death whose sides are lined with the hateful stones.
Does any one going hence expect robes of green beyond,
When these dusky shrouds within the earth have been torn to shreds?
To me thereanent came news, a medley of tangled tales,
By ways that perplex and foil men eager to know the truth.

Ay, short of it fell the Zoroastrian archimage,
The bishop of Christian folk, the rabbin and scribe of Jews,
And wrote legends of their own in volumes which long ago
Have surely been lost, their ink and paper consumed away.
The sects disagreed about the happenings after death,
And those are engulfing seas whereof none may reach the shore.
'Twas said, "Human souls have power and freedom in what they do,"
And some answered, "Nay, 'tis plain they act by necessity."
And oh, had our bodies been created of marble rock,
They scarce had endured the shocks of ever recurring change.

96

With optic glass go question thou the stars that roll o'erhead,
The stars that take away the taste of honey gatherèd:
They point to death, no doubt, but not to rising from the dead.

97

We laugh, but inept is our laughter,
We should weep, and weep sore,
Who are shattered like glass and thereafter
Remoulded no more.

98

Although your mouths hymn Allah One and Peerless,
Your hearts and souls from that ye owe Him shrink.
I swear your Torah gives no light to lead us,
If there 'tis found that wine is lawful drink.

* * * * *

They all err—Moslems, Christians, Jews, and Magians;
Two make Humanity's universal sect:
One man intelligent without religion,
And one religious without intellect.

99

We hope for that world's bliss,
Although our deeds in this
Are not so fair that we should hope Heaven's balconies.

Folk carry not from here
The gauds of wealth and gear,
But laden with their sins depart and disappear.

Reason was dumb. "Ask, then,"
Said I, "the reverend men";
But naught could they decide: this lay beyond their ken.

They talked and lied. When pressed
To put all to the test
Of logic, they broke down in impotence confessed.

100

Falsehood hath so corrupted all the world,
Ne'er deal as true friends they whom sects divide;
But were not hate Man's natural element,
Churches and mosques had risen side by side.

101

(Metre: *Ṭawíl.*)
Oh, cleave ye to Reason's path that rightly ye may be led:
Let none set his hopes except upon the Preserver!
And quench not the Almighty's beams, for lo, He hath given
to all
A lamp of intelligence for use and enjoying.
I see humankind are lost in ignorance: even those
Of ripe age at random guess, like boys playing *mora*.

102

If knowledge aids not me nor baulks my foe,
The losers in Life's game are those who know.
As Allah laid our fortune, so it lies
For ever—O vain wisdom of the wise!

Can this doomed caitiff man, tho' far he fly,
'Scape from his Lord's dominion, earth and sky?
Nay, soon shall we, the hindmost gang, tread o'er
The path our fellow-slaves have trod before.
Surveying humankind, I marvel still
How one thirsts while another drinks his fill.
I draw my bow and every shaft flies wide,
The arrow aimed at me ne'er turns aside.

* * * * *

O fools, awake! The rites ye sacred hold
Are but a cheat contrived by men of old,
Who lusted after wealth and gained their lust
And died in baseness—and their law is dust.

103

Stay at home! No obligation
I account the Pilgrimage,
Lady, on thy sex in virgin
Youth nor yet in wedded age.

Mecca's valley breeds the worst of
Miscreants, who never feel
Fierceness to defend the weaker,
Never flame with knightly zeal.

Men of Shaiba, temple-guardians,
Standing there bemused with wine,
Shove the pilgrim-folk in couples
Through the gateway of the Shrine.

When the people throng around it,
Leave to enter they refuse
None that slips a piece of silver—
Christians jostle in with Jews.

Lady, canst thou do a kindness?
Bless, then, having power to bless,
And if Charity invite thee
To a good act, answer "Yes"!

104

(Metre: *Ṭawíl.*)

I see multitudes that hope the grace of their Lord to win
By kissing a corner-stone or wearing a crucifix.
But pardon me, O my God! At Mecca shall I throw off
Amongst pilgrims newly come the weeds of a widowed frame,
And go down to water-pools along with some fine fellows
From Yemen, who never cared to dig for themselves a well?

105

(Metre: *Basíṭ.*)

Virtue is neither a fast consuming those who it keep,
Nor any office of prayer nor rough fleece wrapped on the limbs.
'Tis nothing but to renounce and cast all evil away
And sweep the breast clear and clean of malice, envy, and spite.
Whate'er the lion profess, no true abstainer is he,
So long as wild beasts and tame fear lest their necks may be broke.

106

Two fates still hold us fast,
A future and a past;
Two vessels' vast embrace
Surrounds us—Time and Space.

Whene'er we ask what end
Our Maker did intend,
Some answering voice is heard
That utters no plain word.

107

If criminals are fated,
'Tis wrong to punish crime.
When God the ores created,
He knew that on a time

They should become the sources
Whence sword-blades dripping blood
Flash o'er the manes of horses
Iron-curbed, iron-shod.

108

Feel shame in presence of the daily sun,
The moon of night, and shining troops untold
Of stars which in the sky their courses hold
By Allah's leave, nor fails them breath to run.

These have a nearer claim and right, I trow,
To reverence than sons of noblest sire.
Glory to Him who made them! Shall their fire
Sink in the dust of Time? I say not so.

Nay, but I muse—Are they endowed with mind
Whereby they can distinguish foul from fair?
Are feminine and masculine up there
By birth related and in marriage joined?

* * * * *

I clean renounce the fool whose hidden track
And open prove him still to error sworn,
Who bans the prayer of afternoon with scorn
And casts the prayer of noon behind his back.

Give the poor man who comes to thee a dole,
Scant though it be, nor frown away thy guest,
But raise for him a flame of ruddy crest
That frolics in the darkness like a foal!

109

'Tis said that spirits remove by transmigration
From body into body, till they are purged;
But disbelieve what error may have urged,
Unless thy mind confirm the information.

Tho' high their heads they carry, like the palm,
Bodies are but as herbs that grow and fade.
Hard polishing wears out the Indian blade,
Allay thy soul's desires and live calm.

110

When the soul leaves
This frame to which it cleaves,
Some say it after grieves.

If with it go
The Reason, it may know
And recollect past woe.

Else, all the reams
O'erwrit with dead men's dreams
Are wasted ink, meseems[1].

111

Ye have gotten a long, long shrift, O kings and tyrants,
And still ye work injustice hour by hour.
What ails you that ye tread no path of glory?
A man may take the field, tho' he love the bower.

But some hope an Imám with voice prophetic
Will rise amidst the silent ranks agaze.
An idle thought! There's no Imám but Reason
To point the morning and the evening ways.

Ḥarírí

Ḥarírí of Baṣra (A.D. 1054–1122) wrote what is, next to the Koran, the most celebrated book in Arabic literature. It is a work of fiction, but one in which the story counts for less than the style. Under the name of al-Ḥárith son of Hammám, Ḥarírí relates the adventures of Abú Zaid, a disreputable old rascal gifted with marvellous powers of improvisation, and withal so genial, humorous, resourceful, and entertaining that we cannot help admiring and even liking him. His character and accomplishments are exhibited in fifty *Maḳámas*, which form not a continuous narrative, but a series of episodes, and are written throughout in rhymed prose and verse. I have translated the eleventh and

[1] The "dead men's dreams" ("ravings," in the original) refer to the descriptions of a future life which occur in the books of Revelation.

twelfth *Maḳámas*—those called after Sáwa and Damascus—imitating their peculiar manner of composition as well as I can.

112

The Maḳáma of Sáwa

Al-Ḥárith son of Hammám related:

Whilst sojourning in Sáwa, I felt my heart was stubborn, slow to melt; so I betook myself to what the Prophet said concerning the heart that is hard, how the cure for it is a visit to the graveyard. And when I arrived at the abode of the dead, of man's dust the common bed, I saw a gathering of people who never stirred beside a newly dug grave, and a corpse being interred; and I turned to join them, meditating on that that cometh at last, and remembering my kinsfolk who had passed. Now, when the grave was filled and the cries of grief were stilled, an old man rose from a mound, leaning on a staff and surveying those around. He had covered his face with his cloak and cunningly disguised his look, and he said, "*They that work, let them work for wages like this*[1]. Gird yourselves, O ye remiss! Bethink yourselves, O ye that take no heed! Consider well, O ye that can mark and read! What ails you? Your peers are buried and your hearts ache not, the mould is poured in and ye quake not; ye reck not of the sudden dooms, ye prepare not for going down into the tombs; though many an eye weeps, ye shed no tears; ye hear the tidings of death with careless ears; the loss of a familiar friend doth not cause you to quail, nor are ye moved when the assembled mourners wail. The bier is carried, and one of you walks behind, but his own house is ever before his mind: he sees his kinsman laid in the dark lair, and all the while he is thinking how he shall get his share; he leaves his comrade for worms to mar, then away he goes with his pipe and guitar. Bitterly have ye grieved if but a grain's weight were chipped from your hoard, yet the cutting off of your loved ones ye have ignored; and ye have been dismayed when ye yourselves fell into trouble, but have made light of it when your kindred were mown down like stubble. Ye have laughed

[1] Koran, XXXVII, 59.

PLATE III

ABÚ ZAID PREACHING IN THE GRAVEYARD AT SÁWA

over him ye came to bury as ye laughed not in the hour of dancing and making merry; and ye have strutted after hearses as ye strutted not on the day ye received a present of purses. Ye have turned from the dirge of the keeners to furnish dinners, and from the anguish of them that mourn their nearest to seek out the viands that are dearest. It seems as if ye were joined to Death by a connexion of protection, or as if from Time's career ye had naught to fear, or as if ye were confident of your safety, and sure that your peace with the Destroyer of delights would endure. Nay, 'tis an ill creed! Nay, but ye will know it, ye will indeed!" Then he recited:

"Pretending sense in vain, how long, O scatterbrain, wilt thou heap sin and bane, and compass error's span?
Thy conscious guilt avow! The white hairs on thy brow admonish thee, and thou hast ears unstopt, O man!
Death's call dost thou not hear? Rings not his voice full clear? Of parting hast no fear, to make thee sad and wise?
How long, sunk in a sea of sloth and vanity, wilt thou play heedlessly, as though Death spared his prize?
Till when, far wandering from virtue, wilt thou cling to evil ways that bring together vice in brief?
For thy Lord's anger shame thou hast none, but let maim o'ertake thy cherished aim, then feel'st thou burning grief.
Thou hail'st with eager joy the coin of yellow die, but if a bier pass by, feigned is thy sorry face;
Perverse and callous wight! thou scornest counsel right to follow the false light of treachery and disgrace.
Thy pleasure thou dost crave, to sordid gain a slave, forgetting the dark grave and what remains of dole;
Were thy true weal descried, thy lust would not misguide, nor thou be terrified by words that should console.
Not tears, blood shall thine eyes pour at the great Assize, when thou hast no allies, no kinsman thee to save;
Straiter thy tomb shall be than needle's cavity: deep, deep thy plunge I see as diver's 'neath the wave.
There shall thy limbs be laid, a feast for worms arrayed, till utterly decayed are wood and bones withal,

Nor may thy soul repel that ordeal horrible, when o'er the Bridge of Hell she must escape or fall.
Astray shall leaders go, and mighty men be low, and sages shall cry, 'Woe like this was never yet.'
Then haste, my thoughtless friend, what thou hast marred to mend, for life draws near its end, and still thou art in the net.
Trust not in fortune, nay, though she be soft and gay; for she will spit one day her venom, if thou dote;
Abate thy haughty pride! lo, Death is at thy side, fastening, whate'er betide, his fingers on thy throat.
When prosperous, refrain from arrogant disdain, nor give thy tongue the rein: a modest tongue is best.
Comfort the child of bale and listen to his tale: repair thine actions frail, and be for ever blest.
Feather the nest once more of those whose little store hath vanished: ne'er deplore the loss nor miser be;
With meanness bravely cope, and teach thine hand to ope, and spurn the misanthrope, and make thy bounty free.
Lay up provision fair and leave what brings thee care: for sea the ship prepare and dread the rising storm.
This, friend, is what I preach, expressed in lucid speech. Good luck to all and each who with my creed conform!"

Then he drew back his sleeve from a fore-arm of strong compacture, on which he had tied the splints of fraud, not of fracture; and set himself to beg audaciously and rapaciously, and beguiled the company by means of that false trimming until his sleeve was full and brimming, when he descended from the mound, rejoicing in the windfall he had found. Said the narrator: I plucked him from behind by the hem of his mantle, and he inclined toward me in humility, and greeted me with civility. And lo, it was our old man, Abú Zaid, with his very eyes and lies, and I said to him:

"How many an artful ruse, O Abú Zaid, wilt use, thy quarry to bemuse? and reck'st thou not of blame?"

His wit flashed, and he answered unabashed:

"Rail not, but understand! Seest thou in any land one that will hold his hand when he can win the game?"

"Get thee gone," said I, "old fiend of the Fire with thy burden dire! There is nothing like thee, for the fairness of thy seeming and the foulness of thy scheming, but dung silver-dight or a privy painted white." So we parted, I to the right and he to the left; and southward I set forth, while he faced the north.

113

The Maḳáma of Damascus

Al-Ḥárith son of Hammám related:

I went from 'Iráḳ to Damascus with its green watercourses, in the day when I had troops of fine-bred horses and was the owner of coveted wealth and resources, free to divert myself, as I chose, and flown with the pride of him whose fullness overflows. When I reached the city after toil and teen on a camel travel-lean, I found it to be all that tongues recite and to contain soul's desire and eye's delight. So I thanked my journey and entered Pleasure's tourney and began there to break the seals of appetites that cloy and cull the clusters of joy, until a caravan for 'Iráḳ was making ready— and by then my wild humour had become steady, so that I remembered my home and was not consoled, but pined for my fold— wherefore I struck the tents of absence and yearning and saddled the steed of returning.

As soon as my companions were arrayed, and the agreement duly made, fear debarred us from setting on our way without an escort to guard us. We sought one in every clan and tried a thousand devices to secure a man, but he was nowhere to be found in the hive: it seemed as though he were not amongst the live. The travellers, being at the end of their tether, mustered at the Jairún gate to take counsel together, and ceased not from tying and unbinding and twisting and unwinding, until contrivance was exhausted and those lost hope who had never lost it.

Now, over against them stood a person of youthful mien, garbed in a hermit's gaberdine: in his hand he held a rosary, while his eyes spake of vigil and ecstasy; at us he was peering, and had sharpened his ear to steal a hearing. When the party was about to scatter, he said to them, for now he had laid open their secret matter, "O people, let your cares be sloughed and your fears rebuffed, for I will safeguard you with that which will cast out dread from your breasts and show itself obedient to your behests." Said the narrator: We demanded of him that he should inform us concerning his gage, and offered him a greater fee than for an embassage; and he declared it was certain words rehearsed to him in a dream of the night, to serve him as a phylactery against the world's despite. Then began we to exchange the furtive glance and wink to one another and look askance. Recognising that we thought poorly of his tale and conceived it to be frail, he said, "Why will ye treat my solemn assurance as an idle toy and my pure gold as alloy? By God, I have traversed many an awesome region and plunged into deadly hazards legion, and it hath enabled me to do without the protection of a guide and to dispense with a quiver at my side. Furthermore, I will banish the suspicion that hath shaken you and remove the distrust that hath o'ertaken you by consorting with you in the desert lands and accompanying you across the Samáwa sands. If my promise prove true, then do ye make my fortune new; but if my lips forswear, then my skin ye may tear and spill my blood and not spare!"

We were inspired to give his vision credit and allow the truth to be as he said it, so we refrained from harrying him, and cast lots for carrying him; and at his bidding we cut the loops of delay and put aside fear of harm or stay. When the pack-saddles were tied and the hour of departure nighed, we begged him to dictate the words of the magic ritual, that we might make them a safeguard perpetual. He said, "Let each one of you repeat the Mother of the Koran[1] at the coming of eve and dawn; then let him say with a tongue of meekness and a voice of weakness, 'O God! O quickener of bodies mouldering

[1] "The Mother of the Koran" is a name given to the first chapter, because it contains the matter or fundamental doctrine of the whole book.

in their site! O averter of blight! O Thou that shieldest from affright! O Thou that dost graciously requite! O refuge of them that sue for favour in Thy sight! O Pardoner and Forgiver by right! Bless Mohammed, the last of Thy prophets for ever, him that came Thy message to deliver! Bless the Lights of his family and the Keys of his victory! And save me, O God, from the intrigues of the satanical and the assaults of the tyrannical; from the vexation of the insolent and the molestation of the truculent; from the oppression of transgressors and the transgression of oppressors; from the foiling of the foilers and the spoiling of the spoilers; from the perfidy of the perfidious and the insidiousness of the insidious! And, O God, protect me from the wrong-doing of them that around me throng and from the thronging around me of them that do me wrong; and keep me from the hands of the injurious, and bring me out of the darkness of the iniquitous, and in Thy mercy let me enter amongst Thy servants that are righteous! O God, preserve me from dangers on my native soil and in the land of strangers, when I roam and come home, when I go in quest and return to rest, in employment and enjoyment, in occupation and vacation! And guard me in myself and my pelf, in my fame and my aim in my weans and my means, in my hold and my fold, in my health and my wealth, in my state and my fate! Let me not decline toward fortune's nadir, or fall under the dominion of an invader, but grant me from Thyself a power that shall be my aider! O God, watch over me with Thine eye and Thine help from on high; and distinguish me by Thy safeguarding and Thy bounteous rewarding; and befriend me with Thy favour and Thy blessing alone, and entrust me not to any care but Thine own! And bestow on me a happiness that decayeth not, and allot to me a comfort that frayeth not; and relieve me from the fears of indigence, and shelter me with the coverlets of affluence; and suffer not the talons of mine enemies to tear, for Thou art He that hearkeneth to prayer.'"

Then he looked down with an unroving eye, and uttered

not a word in reply, so that we said, "An awe hath astounded him, or a faintness hath dumbfounded him." At last he raised his head and heaved his breath and said, "I swear by heaven with its starry train, and by the earth with its highways plain, and by the streaming rain, and by the blazing lamp of the Inane, and by the sounding main, and by the dust-whirling hurricane: truly this is the most auspicious of charms and will stand you in better stead than the men-at-arms: he that cons it at the smiling of the dawn dreads no calamity ere evening's blush comes on; and he that murmurs it to the scouts of darkness as they advance is ensured for the night against any thievish chance."

Said the narrator: So, for our part, we learned it till we knew it by heart, and we repeated it each man to his neighbour, lest we should forget it and lose our labour. Then we marched, speeding the beasts along by prayers, not by the drivers' song, guarding bundle and bale by holy words, not by men in mail; and our friend, although his attention we never lacked, was not claiming the fulfilment of our pact, until, when the house-tops of 'Ána rose in the distance, he cried, "Now, your assistance! your assistance!" whereupon we brought to him of our goods both the concealed and the revealed, and the corded and the sealed, and said, "Take at thy choice, for thou wilt not find amongst us a dissentient voice." But all his delight was for the light and the fine, nothing pleased his eye but the coin: 'twas a full load he shouldered and bore, enough to keep want from his door; then off he skipped as the cutpurse skips, and away he slipped as quicksilver slips. We were distressed by his defaulting and amazed at his bolting, and we sought everywhere for a clue and inquired after him from false guides and true, till we heard that since foot in 'Ána he set he had never quitted the cabaret. The foulness of this rumour egged me on to test the ore of its mine and meddle with what is not in my line. Long before sunrise I repaired to the tavern in disguise, and lo, amidst jars and vats, there was the old varlet in a robe of scarlet, and around him

PLATE IV

ABÚ ZAID CAROUSING IN THE TAVERN AT 'ÁNA

cupbearers beaming and candles gleaming and myrtle and jessamine and pipe and mandolin: now he would be broaching the jars, now waking the music of guitars, now inhaling sweet flower-smells, now sporting with the gazelles. When I struck upon his guileful way and the difference of his to-day from his yesterday, I said, "Woe to thee, O accursed one! So soon hast thou forgotten the day of Jairún?" But he guffawed with a will and began merrily to trill:

"I ride and I ride through the waste far and wide, and I fling away pride to be gay as the swallow;
Stem the torrent's fierce speed, tame the mettlesome steed, that wherever I lead Youth and Pleasure may follow.
I bid gravity pack, and I strip bare my back lest liquor I lack when the goblet is lifted:
Did I never incline to the quaffing of wine, I had ne'er been with fine wit and eloquence gifted.
Is it wonderful, pray, that an old man should stay in a well-stored seray by a cask overflowing?
Wine strengthens the knees, physics every disease, and from sorrow it frees, the oblivion-bestowing!
Oh, the purest of joys is to live sans disguise, unconstrained by the ties of a grave reputation,
And the sweetest of love that the lover can prove is when fear and hope move him to utter his passion.
Thy love then proclaim, quench the smouldering flame, for 'twill spark out thy shame and betray thee to laughter:
Heal the wounds of thine heart and assuage thou the smart by the cups that impart a delight men seek after;
While to hand thee the bowl damsels wait who cajole and enravish the soul with eyes tenderly glancing,
And singers whose throats pour such high-mounting notes, when the melody floats, iron rocks would be dancing!
Obey not the fool who forbids thee to pull beauty's rose when in full bloom thou'rt free to possess it;
Pursue thine end still, though it seem past thy skill: let them say what they will, take thy pleasure and bless it!
Get thee gone from thy sire if he thwart thy desire; spread thy nets nor enquire what the nets are receiving;

But be true to a friend, shun the miser and spend, ways of charity wend, be unwearied in giving.
He that knocks enters straight at the Merciful's gate, so repent or e'er Fate call thee forth from the living!"

I said to him, "Bravo, bravo, for thy recitation, but fie and shame on thy reprobation! By God, whence springeth thy stock? methinks thy riddle is right hard to unlock."

He answered, "I do not wish to explicate but I will indicate:

I am the age's rarity, the wonder of mankind,
I play my tricks amongst them all, and many a dupe I find;
But then I am a needy wretch whom Fortune broke and beat,
And father, too, of little ones laid bare as butcher's meat.
The poor man with a family—none blames him if he cheat."

Said the narrator: Then I knew he was Abú Zaid, the rogue of his race, he that blackens the face of hoariness with disgrace; and I was shocked by the greatness of his iniquity and the abomination of his obliquity. "Old man," I said, "is it not time that thou draw back from thy course of crime?" He growled and scowled and fumed, and pondered a moment and resumed, "'Tis a night for exulting, not for insulting, and an occasion for wine-quaffing, not for mutual scoffing. Away with sorrow till we meet to-morrow!" So I parted from him, in fear of a row, not because I relied on his vow; and I passed my night in the weeds of contrition for having gained admission to the daughter of the vine, not to a mosque or a shrine. And I promised God Almighty that nevermore would I visit a drinking-shop, not though the empire of Baghdád were given me as a sop, and never see the vats of wine again, even if the season of youth might be mine again.

Then we saddled the camels tawny-white in dawn's twilight, and left Abú Zaid in peace with his old tutor, Iblís[1].

[1] Satan.

*Ibnu 'l-Balkhí

The following account of Chosroes Anúsharwán, who reigned in Persia A.D. 531–579, occurs in the *Fársnáma*, a work on the geography of Fárs composed in the first decade of the twelfth century A.D. by a certain Ibnu 'l-Balkhí and dedicated to the Seljúḳ prince, Muḥammad son of Malikshah. The author, who is otherwise unknown, has prefixed to the geographical portion of his work a history of the ancient Persian kings. This is written in slightly archaic but excellent Persian and is well worth reading.

114

Kisrà Anúsharwán the Just

When Kisrà Anúsharwán the Just came to the throne, he set before him (as a pattern) the testaments of Ardashír son of Bábak[1] and fulfilled the precepts contained therein. Wherever he found a book of moral philosophy or politics he used, after reading it, to adopt and put in practice any part of it that pleased him. The principles which he established concerning the kingship, the maintenance of the army, and the administration of justice were such as none of the Persian kings had ever equalled. The tale of his virtues and achievements is too long to relate, and as there is a well-known book on the subject we shall mention only a few of the most important. At the beginning he said, "The empire depends on religion, and until religious affairs are disposed of, no attention can be given to any other affairs. The army must not be in doubt as to its religious belief." Accordingly he summoned his counsellors and in the presence of Buzurjmihr, who was his Vizier, addressed them thus: "Know that this Mazdak is aiming at the sovereignty. My father did not perceive his designs. He is like unto Mání the heretic, whom my ancestor Bahrám son of Hurmuz slew, so that the world was no more troubled by him. Now it is needful to take measures against this man: what course, think ye, is the best?" They all answered, "We are thy slaves, and this thought which thou hast formed is a proof that thy kingdom will endure." Anúsharwán said, "This man hath many followers and great power. He cannot be

[1] The founder of the Sásánian dynasty (A.D. 226–241).

destroyed save by guile, else this will be a long business for us. Now do ye keep the matter secret, that I may find a plan." Thereupon they arose, and Anúsharwán sent a message to Mazdak in these terms: "It is known to me that thou art in the right, and my father was wont to enjoin obedience to thee as a duty. Now it behoves thee to visit me according to thy custom and make known to me the true doctrine and deem that thy place in my favour is as high and firm as it can be." So Mazdak came, and Anúsharwán bestowed on him honours without bound and gave himself up to him in such wise that Mazdak fancied he had entrapped Anúsharwán; and for some time the king was so friendly with him that the people, being unaware of what lay beneath, spoke evil of Anúsharwán, while the missionaries and adherents of Mazdak everywhere raised their heads and carried on their propaganda openly. When Anúsharwán saw that the miscreant had become confident, he said to him one day, "I am disgusted with my retinue and servants and governors and lieutenants and I wish to appoint one of you in the place of each of them. Now write a list of all the notables and soldiers and men of ability and renown amongst thy followers in order that I may appoint every one to a high office and employment; and also a list of the military and civilian classes which are in thy allegiance, that I may confer a kindness and favour upon every man." Mazdak accordingly drew up two lists comprising more than 150,000 men, and then Anúsharwán said: "Mihrján (the autumn festival) is at hand. I desire thee to invite all the missionaries and chiefs and men of renown amongst thy followers, that I may celebrate this festival in their sight and appoint each one to his due office and employment." Mazdak wrote letters to his adherents, bidding them set out for Madá'in (Ctesiphon). Now Anúsharwán had resolved that on the day of Mihrján a great table should be spread, at which he would seat Mazdak and his followers, while he himself stood over Mazdak with a naked weapon in his hand; and that as soon as he killed Mazdak his soldiers should draw the swords concealed in their dress and cut to pieces all those who were seated at the table. This plan having been agreed upon, he despatched *firmáns* to the cities and provinces, enclosing in each a list of the Mazdakites, with orders to seize them all on the day of Mihrján and throw them into prison. When Mihrján came, he commanded that a great table should be spread on the bank of the Tigris, and he caused Mazdak to recline on a cushion and himself stood over him. At the table were seated two thousand Mazdakite missionaries and chiefs, and round Anúsharwán was arrayed a bodyguard of a hundred men with swords hidden in their dress, while the rest of the soldiery surrounded the table on two sides. Anúsharwán had in his hand a battle-axe (*tabarzín*) or, as others say, a halberd (*náchakh*): he was the first to make these weapons, and he devised them to smite Mazdak, for he could not carry a sword. With one blow Anúsharwán struck off Mazdak's head, which fell into his lap; whereupon the soldiers drew their swords and set on those miscreants and destroyed them to the last man. Whosoever of those curs was found in the realm of Chosroes was arrested on the same day. Such as he judged worthy of death he ordered to be killed; the others he imprisoned or pardoned according as he deemed it advisable to deny them liberty or accept their repentance. Thus was the world purged of them. Then having collected their goods and all that Mazdak possessed of treasure, gear, and menials, he ordered that whatever had been taken from the people unjustly, either in the way of communism (*ibáḥat*) or by violence, should be restored to its owners; and in the case of any goods, baggage, or property for which no owner appeared, he commanded that this should be distributed and given to the poor and deserving or used for the defence of the frontiers. He did not let a single *dínár* of all that surplus come into his own treasury, nor did he bestow anything on his soldiers, but expended the whole sum in good works. As regards the women who in the way of communism had fallen into the hands of strangers and had borne children, if the husband wished for his wife she was restored to him, while the children were given to those who most resembled them. When he had finished with the accursed Mazdak and his followers, he turned his attention to the empire and the army. Notwithstanding the eminence and wisdom of Buzurjmihr, who was his Vizier, Anúsharwán arranged so that the secretary (*dabír*) of Buzurjmihr, and likewise his deputy (*ná'ib*), should be able to have free access to the royal presence. With us this *ná'ib* is named the Keeper of the Keys (*kilíd-dár*)[1]; he was called in Pehleví "Íránmázghar[2]," and he acts as the Vizier's deputy. The three ministers in the service of Buzurjmihr were appointed by Anúsharwán himself, and Buzurjmihr had no power to appoint them. What Anúsharwán intended was this: the secretary (*dabír*) was to acquaint him privately with the details of every letter written to great personages or sent to the outlying provinces of the empire; the Keeper of the Keys (*kilíd-dár*) was to give him a true account, face to face, of all that passed whether good or bad, and explain the ways and aspects of policy; and the deputy (*ná'ib*) was to watch over revenue and taxation. These three ministers were men of noble birth, intelligent, accomplished, eloquent, and efficient. Anúsharwán is said to have remarked on one occasion, "The Vizier is like the king's partner: he is invested with authority in government and finance; and these three persons are his hands and his tongue. The King, if he is prudent, will not fail to observe the actions of the Vizier." Again, with this arrangement, the Vizier cannot be defamed and calumniated, and the King is saved from needless anxiety, for if a letter was written accusing the Vizier, the King would question these ministers in secret; if they knew the truth, they would tell it; if not, they would investigate the affair and discover the right and wrong of it. The reason why Anúsharwán several times arrested Buzurjmihr and detained him in custody was that whenever the Vizier conceived some vain project or was minded to play false, his plot was exposed by these three ministers, and the King then sent him to prison before the mischief which he had meditated was irreparable, only releasing him when he had no spirit for intrigue. Buzurjmihr was of noble descent and a member of the royal House, wherefore Anúsharwán regarded him with greater suspicion.

[1] The reading is doubtful.
[2] Probably a corruption of Andarzghar = Counsellor.

In all matters Anúsharwán made excellent dispositions. The Highpriest, whom he appointed to preside over the court of justice, was not surpassed by any of his time in nobility, learning, and piety, and none except the Vizier was held in such reverence as he. Each of the King's ministers was an eminent man of noble race and ancestry and learned withal, who had no superior. Anúsharwán took the utmost care that his courtiers, including his secretary and his chamberlain, should be acute, talented, eloquent and intelligent beyond all others. "The Chamberlain," he said, "is the tongue with which the King speaks to those near him, and the Secretary is the tongue with which he speaks to those far from him: these two ought to be more accomplished and sensible and sagacious than all other men in the world." The Head of the Post and Secret Intelligence held, in his own right, an office of great dignity and was an accomplished nobleman, a master of the pen and perfect in knowledge. Moreover, in every province Anúsharwán had many agents, messengers, and couriers to keep him informed of all that went on and of any new happening, so that he might direct affairs accordingly. By his orders, none but noble and learned men were appointed to office, and he forbade that any base-born person or tradesman or son of a retainer should be instructed in the secretarial art. To set forth all his institutions and reforms would take a long time. He looked into the arrangements concerning the land-tax and found them extremely irregular. Hitherto it had been the custom that in one place the land-tax amounted to a third of the produce, in another place to a fifth, and in some places to no more than a sixth, and for this reason the cultivators were aggrieved. Therefore Anúsharwán, with the consent of the Vizier and the other notables, introduced a system whereby the land-tax was laid upon the people in the following manner:

Cornland. A tax of 1 silver dirhem on every *garí* of land[1].
Land producing rice. A tax of 8 dirhems on every *garí*.
Persian date-palms. A tax of 1 dirhem on every four trees.
Dwarf date-palms. A tax of 1 dirhem on every six trees.
Olive trees. A tax of 1 dirhem on every six trees.

[1] The *garí* or *jaríb* is said to be 3600 square ells.

The poll-tax was collected once a year from those who were liable to pay it, in three grades: 12 dirhems from the rich, 8 from the middle class, and 4 from the lowest. And when Anúsharwán laid down this rule for taxing the land, the burdens of the peasantry were permanently lightened and the kingdom became prosperous and his subjects with one voice bestowed on him the title of "The Just."

*Mu'izzí

Poet-laureate of Sultan Sanjar, the Seljúḳ (A.D. 1092–1157).

115

O thou whose cheeks are the Pleiades and whose lips are coral,
Thy Pleiades are the torment of the heart, thy coral is the food of the soul.
In chase of those Pleiades my back hath become like the sky[1],
For love of that coral my eyes have become like the sea.

Methinks, thy down is a smoke thro' which are seen rose-leaves,
Methinks, thy tresses are a cloud in which is hidden the sun—
A smoke that hath set my stack on fire,
A cloud that hath loosed from mine eyes the rain.

Thine eye, by wounding my heart, hath made me helpless;
Thy tress, by ravishing my soul, hath made me distraught.
If thine eye pierces my heart, 'tis right, for thou art my sweetheart;
And if thy tress ravishes my soul, 'tis fair, for thou art my soul's desire.

In peace, the banquet-hall without thy countenance is not lighted;
In war, the battle-field without thy stature is not arrayed.
The banquet-hall without thy countenance is the sky without the moon;
The battle-field without thy stature is the garden without the cypress.

[1] *I.e.* curved.

My body is in pain from thine eye full of enchantments,
My heart is in sorrow from thy tresses full of guile—
A pain that thy sight turns in a moment to pleasure,
A sorrow that thy speech turns in an instant to joy.

Thy face is a tulip for delicacy and pinkness,
Thy teeth are pearls for brightness and purity.
I never heard of pearls in honey-laden coral,
I never heard of tulips amidst musk-shedding hyacinths[1].

116

If my Belov'd—fair picture!— deigned but to look upon me,
My passion's grief and sorrow were not so sore a burden;
And if her glance tale-telling had not revealed her secret,
From all the world my secret would have been hidden always.
'Twould seem as though I dwelt in a Paradise of gladness,
If now and then my Sweetheart along the road were passing.
O that my food were made of her lips' twin rubies only,
That o'er her in requital mine eye might shed its rubies!
And O that she would never my banquet leave behind her,
That with her cheeks my banquet might glow like beds of tulips!

*'Am'aḳ of Bukhárá

A court-poet. He died in A.D. 1148.

117

O paradisal beauty! come, fetch the cup of wine.
Sweet April hath apparelled the world like Paradise.
The field flings down a carpet of pictured tapestry,
And pridefully the garden puts on a crown of pearls.

A picture of Khawarnaḳ[2] parterre and garden seem,
A satin-woven carpet mountain and meadow-land:
This like a Chinese temple, splendid with China's art;
That like the house of Máni[3], with lovely paintings hung.

[1] "Musk-shedding hyacinths," *i.e.* dark fragrant locks of hair.
[2] A superb castle on the Euphrates.
[3] The Manichaeans attached great importance to calligraphy, and Máni (Manes) himself is believed by the Persians to have been an exquisite artist.

Lo, there the rich tiara of gems on the jasmine-bough!
See how the queenly roses unfold their broideries!
Roses like cheeks of houris, laden with spicy curls;
Jasmines like lawns of Eden, fragrant and beautiful.

As 'twere a bride, the rosebush arrays herself; the cloud
Tirewoman-like is laving the dust and grime away,
Now round her neck arranging a string of pearly tears,
Now drawing o'er her blushes a veil of gauzy mist.

Those tulips, where the cloud's eye hath hid its weeping showers,
Well might'st thou call them flagons of onyx filled with wine,
Or flashes of keen fire in water, or bright waves
Of Badakhsháni ruby tossing in seas of Spring.

*Anwarí

The most renowned of the Persian court-poets (died about A.D. 1190).

118

Unless Fate rules the course of life entire,
Why fall things not according to desire?
To good or evil, as Fate pulls the rein,
So runs the world; and all is planned in vain.

Day after day a thousand pictures pass,
But never Truth appears in Fancy's glass.
"How? Why?" The Painter of these changing scenes,
He works *without* a cause, *without* a means.

Our hands are impotent to loose or bind,
Life's joy and sorrow let us meet resigned.
Beneath yon sky-blue dome our earthly state
Hangs on the order of celestial Fate.

O Time, great lord of Nature! since by thee
My body natural is held in fee,
Why with such eager spite dost thou devise,
Most ancient humpback! torments for the wise?

No mind can reach thy revolution's cause,
No eye discover thy mysterious laws.
From thy dark wheels what anguish o'er me fell
Ah, 'tis a plaint would take long years to tell.

PLATE V

FARÍDU'DDÍN 'AṬṬÁR

119

Yesterday a dear one asked me, "Will you sing of love again?"
Nay, I have done with poetising, fallen from my hand the pen.
Long in error's way I chanted lofty praise and satire stern,
Now those days are gone behind me—vanished never to return.
Love-lay, panegyric, satire, I was making all the three—
Why? Because lust, greed, and anger dwelt unitedly in me:
Lust the livelong night tormenting evermore my sleepless brain
To describe a ringlet's crescent and a lip like sugar-cane;
Greed all day in tribulation pondering o'er a scrap of verse
Where, from whom, and how five dirhems might be coaxed into my purse;
Anger, like a wounded mongrel, solace for his smart would fetch,
Tooth and claw in sullen fury turning on some weaker wretch.
Since the grace of God Almighty shown unto his helpless thrall
Hath unchained me from those harpies—so may He release you all!—
Love-lay, panegyric, satire shall I make now? Heav'n forfend!
I have wronged enough already soul and mind: 'tis time to mend.
Anwarí, beware of boasting!—Honour lays on that a ban—
But when once thy word is plighted, see thou keep it like a man.
From the busy world retired dwell and seek the way that saves!
Very soon the last goes o'er thee of thy life-tide's ebbing waves.

*Farídu'ddín 'Aṭṭár

As a purely mystical poet, 'Aṭṭár (died *circa* A.D. 1225) is excelled in Persia by Jalálu'ddín Rúmí alone. Besides a collection of odes, his poetical works comprise many long *masnavís*, of which the best known is the *Manṭiḳu 'l-Ṭair*; this has been translated into French, under the title of "Le Langage des Oiseaux," by Garcin de Tassy (Paris, 1864). He also wrote in prose the *Tadhkiratu 'l-Auliyá*, the oldest Legend of the Moslem Saints that is extant in Persian. Of its interest to students of mysticism the specimens given below may perhaps be considered a sufficient indication.

120

From the Life of Rábi'a al-'Adawíya

Once in the season of spring she went into her chamber and bowed her head in meditation. Her handmaid said, "O mistress, come forth that thou mayst behold the wondrous works of God!" "Nay," she answered, "do thou come within, that thou mayst behold their Maker. Contemplation of the Maker hath turned me from contemplating that which He made."

It is related that she once fasted seven days and nights, never sleeping, but passing every night in prayer. When she was wellnigh starving, some one came in and left a cupful of food. She went to fetch a lamp, but on returning found that a cat had spilled the cup. "I will go," she said, "and fetch a jug of water and break my fast." While she was fetching it, the lamp went out. She tried to drink in the dark, but the jug slipped from her hand and broke to pieces. She wailed and heaved such a sigh that the room was in danger of catching fire[1]. "O God!" she cried, "what is this Thou art doing to wretched me?" She heard a voice saying, "Lo, if thou wishest, I will bestow on thee the wealth of all the world, but I will remove thy love for Me from thy heart, for heavenly love and earthly wealth cannot meet in one heart. O Rábi'a, thou hast a desire and I have a desire. I and thy desire cannot dwell together in a single heart." Rábi'a said: "When I heard this warning, I cut off my heart from every worldly hope. For thirty years I have prayed as though every prayer that I performed were the last prayer of all, and I have become so detached from mankind that, for fear lest any one should distract my mind from God, I cry at sunrise, 'O God! make me busy with Thee, that they may not make me busy with them.'"

One day Ḥasan of Baṣra and Málik son of Dínár and Shaḳíḳ of Balkh came to see Rábi'a when she was ill. Ḥasan

[1] Because the sigh came from her heart, which was burning with grief.

said, "None is sincere in his claim (to love God) unless he patiently endure the blows of his Lord." Rábi'a said, "This smells of egoism." Shaḳíḳ said, "None is sincere in his claim unless he give thanks for the blows of his Lord." Rábi'a said, "This must be bettered." Málik son of Dínár said, "None is sincere in his claim unless he delight in the blows of his Lord." Rábi'a said, "This still needs to be improved." They said, "Do thou speak." She said, "None is sincere in his claim unless he forget the blows in beholding his Lord."

'Abdu 'l-Wáḥid son of 'Ámir relates that he and Sufyán Thaurí went to ask after Rábi'a in her illness. "She inspired me," he said, "with such awe that I durst not speak, so I begged Sufyán to begin. Sufyán said to Rábi'a, "If thou wouldst utter a prayer, He would relieve thy pain." Rábi'a turned her face towards him and replied, "O Sufyán, dost not thou know who hath willed this pain to me? Hath not God willed it?" Sufyán said, "Yes." "Then," said she, "knowing this, dost thou bid me ask of Him something contrary to His will? It is not right to oppose one's beloved." Sufyán said, "What dost thou desire, O Rábi'a?" She replied, "Why dost thou, who art one of the learned, ask me such a question? By the glory of God, for twelve years I have desired fresh dates and never tasted them, although dates, as thou knowest, are very cheap in Baṣra. I am a servant, and what hath a servant to do with desire? If I will and my Lord will not, 'tis infidelity. Thou must will that which He willeth in order that thou mayst be His true servant. If He Himself give thee aught, that is another thing."

Rábi'a said: "He that worships his Lord either from fear or in hope of recompense is a bad servant." "Why, then," they asked, "dost thou worship Him? Hast thou no hope of Paradise?" She answered, "Is it not enough that we are permitted to worship Him? Ought not we to obey Him, though there were no Paradise and Hell? Is not He worthy of our pure devotion?" And she used to say, "O God! if I worship Thee in fear of Hell, burn me in Hell; and if I worship Thee in hope of Paradise, exclude me from Paradise; but if I worship Thee for Thine own sake, withhold not Thine everlasting beauty!" A man said to Rábi'a, "I have committed many sins: if I were to repent, would God turn towards me?" She replied, "No; but if He were to turn towards thee, thou wouldst repent."

121

From the Life of Dhu 'l-Nún al-Miṣrí

The cause of his conversion was as follows. He received a sign (from Heaven) that he should go to visit such and such an ascetic at such and such a place. He found that this man, having suspended himself from the branch of a tree, was saying, "O body! help me to obey God, or I will keep thee like this until thou diest of hunger." Dhu 'l-Nún began to weep. The ascetic heard him sobbing and cried, "Who is this that pities one whose shame is little and whose sins are great?" Dhu 'l-Nún approached and greeted him and asked what he was doing. He replied that his body would not consent to obey God but desired to mix with mankind. "I thought," said Dhu 'l-Nún, "it must have shed the blood of a Moslem or committed a mortal sin." The ascetic said, "Do not you know that when once you have mixed with mankind, every evil thing will ensue?" "Thou art a fearful ascetic." "If you wish to see one who is more ascetic than I, climb this mountain." Dhu 'l-Nún went up the mountain and saw a young man seated in a cell; one of his feet, which he had cut off, was lying outside and worms were eating it. "One day," he said in answer to Dhu 'l-Nún's question, "I was sitting in this cell, when a woman passed by. My heart inclined to her and my body urged me to follow her. I put one foot outside. I heard a voice saying, 'After having served and obeyed God for thirty years, art not thou ashamed to obey the Devil now?' Thereupon I cut off the foot which I had set outside, and I am waiting here to see what will happen to me. Why have you come to a sinner like me? If you wish to see a man of God, go to the top of the mountain." The mountain was so high that Dhu 'l-Nún could not reach the top, but he inquired about that ascetic and was told that he had long been living in a cell on the highest peak of the mountain; that one day a man disputed with him and declared that daily bread is gained by means of (human) effort; that he then vowed he would never eat anything gained by this means, and that after he had remained without food for some time, God sent bees which flew around him and gave him honey. Dhu 'l-Nún said, "My heart was deeply moved by what I had seen and heard, and I perceived that God takes in hand the affairs of them that put their trust in Him and does not let their tribulation come to naught. Afterwards, as I was going on my way, I saw a little blind bird perched on a tree. It alighted on the ground. I said to myself, 'How does the poor creature get food and drink?' It dug a hole in the earth with its beak, and two basins appeared, one of gold containing sesame and one of silver containing rosewater. The bird ate and drank its fill and flew back to the tree, and the two basins vanished. On seeing this Dhu 'l-Nún became altogether beside himself. He resolved to trust in God and was truly converted. Having gone some distance further, at nightfall he entered a ruined building, where he found a jar of gold and jewels covered by a board on which was inscribed the name of God. His friends divided the gold and jewels, but Dhu 'l-Nún said, "Give me this board, my Beloved's name is upon it"; and he did not cease kissing it all day. Through the blessing thereof he attained to such a degree that one night he dreamed and heard a voice saying to him, "O Dhu 'l-Nún! the others were pleased with gold and precious jewels, but thou wert pleased only with My name: therefore have I opened unto thee the gate of knowledge and wisdom."

They said, "Who is the gnostic?" He replied, "A man of them, apart from them."

He said, "There are three kinds of knowledge of God. Firstly, the knowledge that God is One, which is possessed by all believers; secondly, the knowledge derived from proof and demonstration, which belongs to philosophers, rhetoricians, and theologians; and thirdly, the knowledge of the attributes of the Divine Unity, which belongs to the saints of God, those who behold God with their hearts, in such wise that He reveals unto them what He revealeth not unto any one else in the world."

He said, "Real knowledge is God's illumination of the heart with the pure radiance of knowledge," *i.e.* the sun can be seen only by the light of the sun.

He said, "The more a man knoweth God, the deeper and greater his bewilderment in God"—because the nearer he is to the sun, the more he is dazzled by the sun, until he reaches a point where he is not he.

He was asked concerning the qualities of those who know God. He answered, "The gnostic sees without knowledge, without intuition, without information, without contemplation, without description, without unveiling, and without veil. They are not themselves, and they subsist not through themselves, but in so far as they are themselves they subsist through God. They move as God causes them to move, and their words are the words of God which roll upon their tongues, and their sight is the sight of God which hath entered into their eyes. The Prophet, on whom be peace, told of these qualities when he related that God said, 'When I love a servant, I the Lord am his ear, so that he hears by Me, and his eye, so that he sees by Me, and his tongue, so that he speaks by Me, and his hand, so that he takes by Me.'"

Dhu 'l-Nún said, "On one of my journeys I met a woman and asked her what is the end of love. 'Thou fool!' she cried; 'love hath no end.' I said, 'Why is that?' She answered, 'Because the Beloved is without end.'"

122

From the Life of Báyazíd al-Bisṭámí

One day he was walking with a number of his disciples. The path was very narrow. He saw a dog coming along and turned back to let it pass. One of his disciples blamed him secretly and thought to himself, "How can Báyazíd, who is the king of gnostics, make way for a dog?" Báyazíd said, "This dog asked me with dumb eloquence, saying, 'In the eternal past what fault did I commit, and what act of grace didst thou perform, that I am clad in the skin of a dog, while the robe of spiritual royalty hath been conferred on thee?' This thought came into my head and I made way for the dog."

It is related that he said, "A man met me on the road and asked whither I was going. I said, 'To make the Pilgrimage.' 'What money have you?' 'Two hundred dirhems.' 'Give them to me,' he said, 'for I have a wife and children, and walk round me seven times: this will be your Pilgrimage.' I did so and returned home."

Some one went to the door of Báyazíd's house and shouted. "Whom are you seeking?" said he. "Báyazíd." The Shaikh said, "Poor Báyazíd! For thirty years I have been seeking Báyazíd and have not yet discovered any trace of him." When this saying was repeated to Dhu 'l-Nún, he exclaimed, "God forgive my brother Báyazíd! for he is lost with those who have become lost in God."

He said, "I came forth from Báyazíd-ness as a snake from its skin. Then I looked. I saw that lover, beloved, and love are one; for in the world of unification all can be one."

He said, "I went from God to God, until they cried from me in me, 'O Thou I!'"

He said, "Nothing is better for a man than to be without aught, having no asceticism, no theory, no practice. When he is without all, he is with all."

One day he was speaking of the Truth and was sucking his lip and saying, "I am the wine-drinker and the wine and the cup-bearer." He said, "Thirty years the high God was my mirror, now I am my own mirror"—*i.e.* "that which I was I am no more, for 'I' and 'God' is a denial of the Unity of God. Since I am no more, the high God is His own mirror. Lo, I say that God is the mirror of my own self, for He speaks with my tongue and I have vanished."

He said, "For a long while I used to circumambulate the Ka'ba. When I attained unto God, I saw the Ka'ba circumambulating me."

He said, "For thirty years I used to say, 'Do this' and 'Give this,' but when I reached the first stage of gnosis, I said, 'O God, be Thou mine and do whatsoever Thou wilt.'"

He said, "The gnostic's lowest rank is this, that the attributes of God are in him."

He said, "A single atom of the sweetness of gnosis in a man's heart is better than a thousand pavilions in Paradise."

He said, "Gnostics are a boon to Paradise, and Paradise is a bane to them."

He said, "It is impossible that any one should know God and not love Him; and knowledge without love is worthless."

Báyazíd was asked, "What is the chief sign of the gnostic?" He replied, "That while he eats with thee he flees from thee, and while he buys from thee and sells to thee his heart is in the gardens of holiness, reclining on the pillow of communion."

He said, "Men learn from the dead, but I learn from the Living One who never dies. All the rest speak *to* God, but I speak *from* God. Nothing is harder to me than the pursuit of (exoteric) knowledge."

He said, "If the Eight Paradises were unfolded in my hut, and if the Two Worlds were offered to me as my fief, I would not give in exchange for them one sigh that rises from my soul at dawn when I remember my longing for Him."

He said, "People fancy that the way to God is clearer than the sun, but all these years I have been wishing that God would reveal to me as much as a needle's point of this way, and I have wished in vain."

He said, "All that exists is gained in two steps: by lifting up the foot from self-interest and setting it down on the commandments of God."

He said, "This thing we tell of can never be found by seeking, yet only seekers find it."

He was asked, "What is the way to God?" He replied, "Leave the way and you have attained to God."

It is related that he was asked, "How didst thou gain this rank, and by what means didst thou win unto this station?" He answered, "One night in my boyhood I came forth from Bisṭám. The moon was shining and everything was still. I beheld a Presence beside which the eighteen thousand worlds appeared as an atom. Agitation fell upon me and a mighty emotion overwhelmed me. I cried, 'O Lord! a court of this grandeur, and so empty! Works of this sublimity, and such loneliness!' Then a voice came from Heaven, saying, 'The court is empty, not because none comes, but because We do not will; since it is not every one with face unwashed that is worthy to enter this court.'"

He said, "If I am asked in the place of Judgment why I have *not* done something, I shall be more pleased than if I am asked why I have done something"—*i.e.* "there is egoism in every act of mine, and egoism is dualism, and dualism is worse than sin, except as regards a pious act that is done upon me and in which I have no part."

He said, "Forgetfulness of self is remembrance of God. Whoever knows God through God becomes living, and whoever knows God through self becomes dead."

He said, "I wished to know what is the sorest punishment suffered by the body. I perceived that nothing is worse than forgetfulness (of God). Hell-fire does not inflict so much pain as a single mote of forgetfulness."

Some one asked him why he did not pray during the night. He answered, "I have no leisure to pray: I am roaming the spiritual world, and whenever I see any one fallen I help him to rise"—*i.e.* "I am at work within."

He said, "Any one whose reward from God is deferred until to-morrow (the Day of Judgment) has not truly worshipped Him to-day, since every moment of self-mortification is rewarded immediately."

He said, "Endeavour to gain one moment in which thou seest only God in earth and heaven."

They asked his age. "Four years," he replied. They said, "How is that?" He answered, "Seventy years I was shrouded in the veils of this world, but since four years I have been beholding Him—ah, do not ask me how! Time without vision is not a part of life."

He was asked concerning the command to do good and shun evil. He answered, "Be in a domain where neither of these things exists: both of them belong to the world of created beings; in the presence of Unity there is neither command nor prohibition."

He said, "All this talk and turmoil and noise and movement and desire is outside of the veil; within the veil is silence and calm and rest."

He said, "Dost thou hear how there comes a voice from the brooks of running water? But when they reach the sea they are quiet, and the sea is neither augmented by their in-coming nor diminished by their out-going."

IBNU 'L-FÁRIḌ

'UMAR IBNU 'L-FÁRIḌ, the greatest of the Arabic mystical poets, died at Cairo in A.D. 1235. His odes, though few in number, are unique in quality. The longest of them describes his inner life, sets forth the way to oneness with God, and depicts the nature of that oneness so far as it can be put into words. From this poem I have taken the fine passage in which the relation of the soul to phenomena is compared with that of the showman of the shadow-play to the puppets which he, hidden behind a screen, displays in every variety of action. The odes of Ibnu 'l-Fáriḍ are discussed in *Studies in Islamic Mysticism*, pp. 162–266.

123

Let passion's swelling tide my senses drown!
Pity love's fuel, this long-smouldering heart,
Nor answer with a frown,
When I would fain behold Thee as Thou art,
"*Thou shalt not see Me*[1]." O my soul, keep fast
The pledge thou gav'st: endure unfaltering to the last!
For Love is life, and death in love the Heaven
Where all sins are forgiven.
To those before and after and of this day,
That witnesseth my tribulation, say,
"By me be taught, me follow, me obey,
And tell my passion's story through wide East and West."
With my Beloved I alone have been
When secrets tenderer than evening airs
Passed, and the Vision blest
Was granted to my prayers,
That crowned me, else obscure, with endless fame,
The while amazed between
His beauty and His majesty
I stood in silent ecstasy,
Revealing that which o'er my spirit went and came.
Lo, in His face commingled
Is every charm and grace;
The whole of Beauty singled
Into a perfect face
Beholding Him would cry,
"There is no God but He, and He is the most High!"

[1] As God said to Moses (Koran, VII, 139).

124

Where eyes encounter souls in battle-fray,
I am the murdered man whom 'twas no crime to slay.
At the first look, ere love in me arose,
To that all-glorious beauty I was vowed.
God bless a racked heart crying,
And lids that passion will not let me close,
And ribs worn thin,
Their crookedness wellnigh to straightness shaped
By the glow within,
And seas of tears whence I had never 'scaped
But for the fire of sighing!
How sweet are maladies which hide
Me from myself, my loyal proofs to Love!
Though after woeful eve came woeful dawn,
It could not move
Once to despair my spirit: I never cried
To Agony, "Begone!"
I yearn to every heart that passion shook,
And every tongue that love made voluble,
And every deaf ear stopped against rebuke,
And every lid not dropped in slumbers dull.
Out on a love that hath no melting eyes!
Out on a flame from which no rapture flies!

125

Feign coy disdain, for well art thou entitled;
And domineer, for Beauty hath given thee power.
Thine is the word: then will whatso thou willest,
Since over me Beauty hath made thee ruler.
If in death I shall be with thee united,
Hasten it on, so may I be thy ransom!
And try, in all ways thou deem'st good, my passion,
For where thy pleasure is, my choice attends it.
Whate'er betide, thou to myself art nearer
Than I, since but for thee I had not existed.
Not of thy peers am I: enough of glory,
That loving thee I bow in lowly worship.

And though I claim not—'twere too high relation—
Favour with thee, and thou in truth my Master,
Yet me sufficeth to be thought to love thee
And counted by my folk amongst thy slain ones.
Yea, in this tribe thou own'st a dead man, living
Through thee, who found it sweet to die for love's sake;
A slave and chattel who never pined for freedom
Nor, hadst thou left, would let thee leave him lonely;
Whom beauty veiled by awe doth so enravish,
He feels delicious even that veil of torment,
When thou, brought nigh to him by hope's assurance,
Art borne afar by fear of sundering darkness.
Now, by his ready advance when thee he visits,
By his alarmed retreat when thou affright'st him,
I swear mine heart is melted: oh, allow it
To crave thee whilst it hath of hope a remnant;
Or bid sleep (yet, methinks, 'twill disobey thee,
Obedient else) pass o'er mine eyelids lightly;
For in a dream, perchance, will rise before me
Thy phantom and reveal to me a mystery.

126

Lo, from behind the veil mysterious
The forms of things are shown in every guise
Of manifold appearance; and in them
An all-wise providence hath joined what stands
Opposed in nature: mute they utter speech,
Inert they move and void of splendour shine[1].
And so it comes that now thou laugh'st in glee,
Then weep'st anon, like mother o'er dead child,
And mournest, if they sigh, for pleasure lost,
And tremblest, if they sing, with music's joy[2].
Birds warbling on the boughs delight thine ear,
The while their sweet notes sadden thee within;

[1] "The forms of things," *i.e.* the puppets shown by means of the shadow-lantern, typify phenomena, which in themselves are lifeless and passive: all their life and activity is the effect of the manifestation in them of the actions and attributes of Reality.

[2] The scenes and incidents of the shadow-play arouse various emotions in the spectators.

Thou wonderest at their voices and their words—
Expressive unintelligible tongues!
On land the camels cross the wilderness,
At sea the ships run swiftly through the deep;
And thou behold'st two armies—one on land,
On sea another—multitudes of men,
Clad, for their bravery, in iron mail
And fenced about with points of sword and spear.
The land-troops march on horseback or on foot,
Bold cavaliers and stubborn infantry;
The warriors of the sea some mount on deck,
Some climb the masts like lances straight and tall.
Here in assault they smite with gleaming swords,
There thrust with tough brown shafts of quivering spears;
Part drowned with fire of arrows shot in showers,
Part burned with floods of steel that pierce like flames;
These rushing onward, offering their lives,
Those reeling broken 'neath the shame of rout;
And catapults thou seest hurling stones
Against strong fortresses and citadels,
To ruin them. And apparitions strange
Of naked viewless spirits thou mayst espy[1],
That wear no friendly shape of humankind,
For genies love not men.
And in the stream
The fisher casts his net and draws forth fish;
And craftily the fowler sets a snare
That hungry birds may fall in it for corn.
And ravening monsters wreck the ships at sea,
And lions in the jungle rend their prey,
And in the air some birds, and in the wilds
Some animals, hunt others. And thou seest
Many a form besides, whose names I pass,
Putting my trust in samples choice, tho' few.

Regard now what is this that lingers not
Before thine eye and in a moment fades.

[1] The genies (*Jinn*) are described as ethereal creatures, endowed with speech, transparent (so that they are normally invisible), and capable of assuming various shapes.

All thou beholdest is the act of one
In solitude, but closely veiled is he.
Let him but lift the screen, no doubt remains:
The forms are vanished, he alone is all;
And thou, illumined, knowest that by his light
Thou find'st his actions in the senses' night.

Ibnu 'l-'Arabí

None of the Mohammedan mystics is more celebrated than Muḥyi'ddín Ibnu 'l-'Arabí, who was born in A.D. 1165 at Murcia in Spain and died in A.D. 1240 at Damascus. He was a most prolific and original writer and exerted a profound influence on Moslem and, to some extent, on medieval Christian religious philosophy—*e.g.* on the speculations of "the Illuminated Doctor," Raymond Lull.

127

When God willed in respect of His Beautiful Names (attributes), which are beyond enumeration, that their essences—or if you wish, you may say "His essence"—should be seen, He caused them to be seen in a microcosmic being which, inasmuch as it is endowed with existence, contains the whole object of vision, and through which the inmost consciousness of God becomes manifested to Him[1]. This He did, because the vision that consists in a thing's seeing itself by means of itself is not like its vision of itself in something else that serves as a mirror for it: therefore God appears to Himself in a form given by the place in which He is seen (*i.e.*, the mirror), and He would not appear thus (objectively) without the existence of this place and His epiphany to Himself therein. God had already brought the universe into being with an existenc resembling that of a fashioned soulless body, and it was li!.: an unpolished mirror. Now, it belongs to the Divine decree (of creation) that He did not fashion any place but such as must of necessity receive a Divine soul, which God has described as having been breathed into it; and this denotes the acquisition by that fashioned form of capacity to receive the emanation, *i.e.*, the perpetual self-manifestation which has never ceased and never shall. It

[1] See *Studies in Islamic Mysticism*, p. 82 foll., and pp. 106–107.

remains to speak of the recipient (of the emanation). The recipient proceeds from naught but His most holy emanation, for the whole affair (of creation) begins and ends with Him: to Him it shall return, even as from Him it began.

The Divine will (to display His attributes) entailed the polishing of the mirror of the universe. Adam (the human essence) was the very polishing of that mirror and the soul of that form, and the angels are some of the faculties of that form, *viz.*, the form of the universe which the Ṣúfís in their technical language describe as the Great Man, for the angels in relation to it are as the spiritual and corporeal faculties in the human organism....The aforesaid microcosmic being is named a Man and a Vicegerent. He is named a Man on account of the universality of his organism and because he comprises all realities. Moreover, he stands to God as the pupil, which is the instrument of vision, to the eye; and for this reason he is named a Man[1]. By means of him God beheld His creatures and had mercy on them[2]. He is Man, the originated (in his body), the eternal (in his spirit); the organism everlasting (in his essence), the Word that divides and unites. The universe was completed by his existence, for he is to the universe what the bezel is to the seal—the bezel whereon is graven the signature that the King seals on his treasuries. Therefore He named him a Vicegerent, because he guards the creatures (of God) just as the King guards his treasuries by sealing them; and so long as the King's seal remains on them, none dares to open them save by his leave. God made him His Vicegerent in the guardianship of the universe, and it continues to be guarded whilst this PERFECT MAN is there. Dost not thou see that when he shall depart (to the next world) and his seal shall be removed from the treasury of this world, there shall no more remain in it that which God stored therein, but the treasure shall go forth, and every type shall return to its (ideal) antitype, and all existence shall be transferred to the next world and sealed on the treasury of the next world for ever and ever?

[1] The pupil of the eye is named in Arabic *insán*, which also signifies "man."

[2] By bringing them into existence.

128

The believer praises the God who is in his form of belief and with whom he has connected himself. He praises none but himself, for his God is made by himself, and to praise the work is to praise the maker of it: its excellence or imperfection belongs to its maker. For this reason he blames the beliefs of others, which he would not do, if he were just. Beyond doubt, the worshipper of this particular God shows ignorance when he criticises others on account of their beliefs. If he understood the saying of Junaid, "The colour of the water is the colour of the vessel containing it[1]," he would not interfere with the beliefs of others, but would perceive God in every form and in every belief. He has opinion, not knowledge: therefore God said, "I am in My servant's opinion of Me," *i.e.*, "I do not manifest Myself to him save in the form of his belief." God is absolute or restricted, as He pleases; and the God of religious belief is subject to limitations, for He is the God who is contained in the heart of His servant. But the absolute God is not contained by any thing, for He is the being of all things and the being of Himself, and a thing is not said either to contain itself or not to contain itself.

129

My heart is capable of every form:
A cloister for the monk, a fane for idols,
A pasture for gazelles, the votary's Ka'ba,
The tables of the Torah, the Koran.
Love is the faith I hold: wherever turn
His camels, still the one true faith is mine.

130

A diver, who essayed to bring to shore the red jacinth of Deity hidden in its resplendent shell, emerged from that ocean empty-handed, with broken arms, blind, dumb, and

[1] *I.e.*, God is revealed in different forms of belief according to the capacity of the believer. The mystic alone sees that He is One in all forms, for the mystic's heart is all-receptive: it assumes whatever form God reveals Himself in, as wax takes the impression of the seal.

dazed. When he regained his breath and when his senses were no longer obscured, he was asked, "What hath disturbed thee and what is this thing that hath befallen thee?" He answered, "Far is that which ye seek! Remote is that which ye desire! None ever attained unto God, and neither spirit nor body conceived the knowledge of Him. He is the Glorious One who is never reached, the Being who possesses but is not possessed. Inasmuch as before His attributes the mind is distraught and the reason totters, how can they attain unto His very essence?"

131

The child affects the father's disposition, so that he descends from his authority and plays with him and prattles to him and brings his mind down to the child's, for unconsciously he is under his sway; then he becomes engrossed with educating and protecting his child and with seeking what is good for him and amusing him, that he may not be unhappy. All this is the work of the child upon the father and is owing to the power of his state, for the child was with God a short while ago, having newly come into the world, whereas the father is further away; and one that is further from God is subject to one that is nearer to Him.

*Jalálu'ddín Rúmí

The leading mystical poet of Persia and founder of the Mevleví order of dervishes. He died at Ḳoniya (Iconium) in Galatia in A.D. 1273. Of the pieces translated, the last three are taken from the *Masnaví*. The rest belong to the collection of odes entitled *Díwán-i Shams-i Tabríz*, which he composed in the name of Shamsu'ddín of Tabríz, his spiritual preceptor.

132

He comes, a moon whose like the sky ne'er saw, awake or dreaming,
Crowned with eternal flame no flood can lay.
Lo, from the flagon of thy love, O Lord, my soul is swimming,
And ruined all my body's house of clay!

When first the Giver of the grape my lonely heart befriended,
Wine fired my bosom and my veins filled up;
But when his image all mine eye possessed, a voice descended:
"Well done, O sovereign Wine and peerless Cup!"

Love's mighty arm from roof to base each dark abode is hewing
Where chinks reluctant catch a golden ray.
My heart, when Love's sea of a sudden burst into its viewing,
Leaped headlong in, with "Find me now who may!"

As, the sun moving, clouds behind him run,
All hearts attend thee, O Tabríz's Sun!

133

Poor copies out of heaven's original,
Pale earthly pictures mouldering to decay,
What care although your beauties break and fall,
When that which gave them life endures for aye?

Oh, never vex thine heart with idle woes:
All high discourse enchanting the rapt ear,
All gilded landscapes and brave glistering shows
Fade—perish, but it is not as we fear.

Whilst far away the living fountains ply,
Each petty brook goes brimful to the main.
Since brook nor fountain can for ever die,
Thy fears how foolish, thy lament how vain!

What is this fountain, wouldst thou rightly know?
The Soul whence issue all created things.
Doubtless the rivers shall not cease to flow,
Till silenced are the everlasting springs.

Farewell to sorrow, and with quiet mind
Drink long and deep: let others fondly deem
The channel empty they perchance may find,
Or fathom that unfathomable stream.

The moment thou to this low world wast given,
A ladder stood whereby thou mightst aspire;
And first thy steps, which upward still have striven,
From mineral mounted to the plant: then higher

To animal existence: next, the Man,
With knowledge, reason, faith. O wondrous goal!
This body, which a crumb of dust began—
How fairly fashioned the consummate whole!

Yet stay not here thy journey: thou shalt grow
An angel bright and home far off in heaven.
Plod on, plunge last in the great Sea, that so
Thy little drop make oceans seven times seven.

"The Son of God!" Nay, leave that word unsaid,
Say, "God is One, the pure, the single Truth."
What though thy frame be withered, old, and dead,
If the soul keep her fresh immortal youth?

134

Lo, for I to myself am unknown, now in God's name what must I do?
I adore not the Cross or the Crescent, I am not a Giaour or a Jew.
East nor West, land nor sea is my home, I have kin nor with angel nor gnome,
I am wrought not of fire or of foam, I am shaped not of dust or of dew.
I was born not in China afar, not in Saḳsín and not in Bulghár;
Not in India, where five rivers are, or 'Iráḳ or Khurásán I grew.
Not in this world or that world I dwell, not in Paradise, neither in Hell;
Not from Eden and Riẕwán I fell, not from Adam my lineage I drew.
In a place beyond uttermost place, in a tract without shadow of trace,
Soul and body transcending I live in the soul of my Loved One anew!

135

If there be any lover in the world, O Moslems, 'tis I.
If there be any believer, infidel, or Christian hermit, 'tis I.
The wine-dregs, the cupbearer, the minstrel, the harp and the music,
The beloved, the candle, the drink and the joy of the drunken—'tis I.
The two-and-seventy creeds and sects in the world
Do not really exist: I swear by God that every creed and sect—'tis I.
Earth and air and water and fire—knowest thou what they are?
Earth and air and water and fire, nay, body and soul too—'tis I.
Truth and falsehood, good and evil, ease and difficulty from first to last,
Knowledge and learning and asceticism and piety and faith—'tis I.
The fire of Hell, be assured, with its flaming limbos,
Yes, and Paradise and Eden and the houris—'tis I.
This earth and heaven with all that they hold,
Angels, peris, genies, and mankind—'tis I.

136

Up, O ye lovers, and away! 'Tis time to leave the world for aye.
Hark, loud and clear from heaven the drum of parting calls—let none delay!
The cameleer hath risen amain, made ready all the camel-train,
And quittance now desires to gain: why sleep ye, travellers, I pray?
Behind us and before there swells the din of parting and of bells;
To shoreless Space each moment sails a disembodied spirit away.

From yonder starry lights, and through those curtain-awnings darkly blue,
Mysterious figures float in view, all strange and secret things display.
From this orb, wheeling round its pole, a wondrous slumber o'er thee stole:
O weary life that weighest naught, O sleep that on my soul dost weigh!
O heart, toward thy heart's love wend, and O friend, fly toward the Friend,
Be wakeful, watchman, to the end: drowse seemingly no watchman may.

137

Happy the moment when we are seated in the palace, thou and I,
With two forms and with two figures but with one soul, thou and I.
The colours of the grove and the voice of the birds will bestow immortality
At the time when we come into the garden, thou and I.
The stars of heaven will come to gaze upon us:
We shall show them the moon herself, thou and I.
Thou and I, individuals no more, shall be mingled in ecstasy,
Joyful and secure from foolish babble, thou and I.
All the bright-plumed birds of heaven will devour their hearts with envy
In the place where we shall laugh in such a fashion, thou and I.
This is the greatest wonder, that thou and I, sitting here in the same nook,
Are at this moment both in 'Irák and Khurásán, thou and I.

138

Why wilt thou dwell in mouldy cell, a captive, O my heart?
Speed, speed the flight! a nursling bright of yonder world thou art.
He bids thee rest upon his breast, he flings the veil away:
Thy home wherefore make evermore this mansion of decay?

Oh, contemplate thy true estate, enlarge thyself, and rove
From this dark world, thy prison, whirled to that celestial grove.
O honoured guest at Love's high feast, O bird of the angel-sphere,
'Tis cause to weep if thou wilt keep thy habitation here.
A voice at morn to thee is borne—God whispers to the soul—
"If on the way the dust thou lay, thou soon wilt gain the goal."
That road be thine toward the Shrine! and lo, in bush and briar
The many slain by love and pain in flower of young desire,
Who on the track fell wounded back, and saw not ere the end
A ray of bliss, a touch, a kiss, a token of the Friend!

139

He is the source of evil, as thou sayest,
Yet evil hurts Him not. To make that evil
Denotes in Him perfection. Hear from me
A parable. The heavenly Artist paints
Beautiful shapes and ugly: in one picture
The loveliest women in the land of Egypt
Gazing on youthful Joseph amorously;
And lo, another scene by the same hand,
Hell-fire and Iblís with his hideous crew:
Both master-works, created for good ends,
To show His perfect wisdom and confound
The sceptics who deny His mastery.
Could He not evil make, He would lack skill:
Therefore He fashions infidel alike
And Moslem true, that both may witness bear
To Him, and worship One Almighty Lord.

140

Fools buy false coins because they are like the true.
If in the world no genuine minted coin
Were current, how would forgers pass the false?
Falsehood were nothing unless truth were there

To make it specious. 'Tis the love of right
Lures men to wrong. Let poison but be mixed
With sugar, they will cram it into their mouths.
Oh, cry not that all creeds are vain! Some scent
Of truth they have, else they would not beguile.
Say not, "How utterly fantastical!"
No fancy in the world is all untrue.
Amongst the crowd of dervishes hides one,
One true fakir. Search well and thou wilt find!

141

I died as mineral and became a plant,
I died as plant and rose to animal,
I died as animal and I was man.
Why should I fear? When was I less by dying?
Yet once more I shall die as man, to soar
With angels blest; but even from angelhood
I must pass on: all except God doth perish.
When I have sacrificed my angel soul,
I shall become what no mind e'er conceived.
Oh, let me not exist! for Non-existence
Proclaims in organ tones, "*To Him we shall return*[1]."

*SA'DÍ OF SHÍRÁZ

THE author of the *Gulistán* and *Bústán* is too well known to require an introduction here. His character has been admirably sketched by Professor Browne (*Literary History of Persia*, vol. II, p. 530 foll.), who remarks that "his real charm and the secret of his popularity lie not in his consistency but in his catholicity; in his works is matter for every taste, the highest and the lowest." It might be added that, whatever he touches either in prose or verse, he has the art of making it as agreeable as is possible.

With noble pity old Firdausi sings
The fate of heroes and the fall of kings.
Nizami next did warmer genius move
To paint the subtle lunacy of love,
Till Sa'di took the pencil and began
A vaster theme, a worthier subject—Man.

[1] Koran, II, 151.

O full of human wisdom, happy sage,
A Persian Horace, mingling on thy page,
Where childhood learns to read, age reads to learn,
Moral with gay and tale with truth in turn;
Which, as we read, our fancy so beguile,
The matter pleases for the golden style,
A style that softly winning, simply drest,
Endears the topic and refines the jest[1].

Sa'dí died in A.D. 1291. I have translated part of the preface to the *Gulistán*, a vivid passage of autobiography from the *Bústán*, and a few of the Odes. Sa'dí's odes, which are now being edited by Sir Lucas King, are graceful and attractive but not to be compared, in my opinion, with those of Ḥáfiẓ. Even in his lyrical poetry, he often reminds us that he was less a dervish and mystic than a moralist and man of the world.

142

The Preface to the Gulistán (*Rose-garden*)

In the name of God the merciful and compassionate: Praise to the great and glorious God! We approach Him by worship and increase our blessings by thanksgiving. Every breath, as it is drawn in, helps to sustain life, and in being sent forth exhilarates the body, so that in every breathing are two blessings; and for each blessing an acknowledgement is due.

Whose hand or tongue may quit the fee,
O Lord, of thanksgiving to Thee?

The showers of His infinite mercy reach every place, and everywhere is spread the table of His unstinted grace; He does not rend the veil of His servants' honour albeit foul sin they devise, or withhold the daily bread of His creatures for a trespass hateful in His eyes.

O bounteous Giver, from whose hidden store
To Guebre and Christian nourishment descends,
If thus Thine enemies are provided for,
How canst Thou ever disappoint Thy friends?

[1] These lines were written about twenty-five years ago when I had begun a translation of the *Gulistán*, which is likely to remain unfinished.

At His word the zephyr unfolds a carpet of emerald on the plain, and the tender plants in their earthen cradle are nursed by the rain; the trees, to celebrate the New Year, in richly woven silk are gowned and the young boughs garlanded with blossom when the Spring Festival comes round; by His might the juice of the vine exceedeth honey in balm, and the date-stone by the blessing of His upbringing towers into the palm.

For us, to earn our bread, the cloud, the breeze,
Sun, moon, and sky with busy motion toil,
That we may eat, remembering God the while:
Should Man serve less obediently than these?

'Tis delivered in tradition from the principal of beings, the pride of creation, the mercy of mankind, the quintessence of mortality, the completer of the cycle of prophecy, Mohammed the Chosen—God bless him and give him peace!—that whenever a sinful wretch lifts up his hands in supplication to the court of God Almighty, He regards him not. Again he cries out, and again God turns away. Yet again he cries out with humble entreaty and lamentation: the Lord saith, "O Mine angels, I am ashamed before My servant, for he hath none other but Me. Verily, I have pardoned him."

Look now, the Lord's sweet charity!
His servant sins, ashamed is He.

They that are vowed to the Temple of His glory confess the shortcoming of their devotion, saying, "We have not worshipped Thee duly"; and they that laud the splendour of His beauty fall into bewilderment, saying, "We have not known Thee truly."

Ask me not His description! Nay, for how,
How might I senseless of the Signless speak?
We lovers are the slain of the Beloved,
'Tis idle of the slain a voice to seek.

A certain mystic had bowed his head in holy meditation and plunged deep in the sea of divine vision. When he came back to himself, one of his companions said pleasantly, "What gift dost thou bring to us from the garden where thou hast been?" He answered, "It was in my mind, when I saw the rose-bush, to fill my skirt with roses and bring them home to you, but their perfume so enravished me that my skirt slipped from my hand."

O nightingale, learn of the moth to love,
That shrivels in the flame without a sigh.
They know not Thee, whom they pretend it of;
Who knows indeed, knows naught eternally.
Beyond imagination Thou dost move,
Higher than all is said, writ, heard of high;
And so, when life has ebbed and we depart,
The first poor line of Thee is all our art.

The Author says of his reason for making this book

One evening I was thinking over bygone days and regretting a life wasted in foolish ways, piercing the stone of my heart with the diamond of tears, and reciting these verses which the occasion commended to mine ears:

Each moment steals a breath of life once more,
And few, I see, are now remaining o'er.
What! Fifty years by lethargy possessed!—
Yet mayst thou realise the fleeting rest.
Shame on the unready traveller, who is racked
When drum-call finds him with his load unpacked,
Or, though his journey might have been begun,
Lies fast asleep beneath the rising sun.
Successive mortals each a fabric build
And vacant leave to others what they filled;
In turn those others like ambition fires,
But none at last accomplished his desires.
Ah, dote not on the World—the treacherous jade
To merit true affection is not made.
How transitory is peace amongst the four
Unbridled humours, with themselves at war!
And if so be that one the mastery win,
Up flies the fair soul to her heavenly kin.
Can wise hearts ever take the world to wife?
Can pure minds linger in the embrace of life?
Since good with evil must go down to earth,

Happy are they who shine in modest worth.
Oh, send provision for the life to come
(For none will bring it after) to thy tomb!
Good man, be not deceived. Like summer snow
Thy days are melting, thou hast few to go;
And if to market empty hands thou bear,
Thou'lt fetch no turban home, alas, from there.
Who eats his corn whilst yet the blade is green,
At harvest he a crop of husks will glean.
To Sa'dí's counsel lend a heedful ear.
This is the way. Step forward! Never fear!

Having considered of the matter, I resolved to make solitude my vocation and withdraw from conversation; to blot out the record of my vanities and speak no further inanities.

Better sit, dumb and deaf, aside
Than wag a tongue thou canst not guide.

I had a bosom-friend who bore in my sorrows an equal share and companioned me in care. It chanced that he came to see me, as he was in the way of doing; but although his mirth would have invited me and his playfulness delighted me, I answered not so much as yea and nay, nor lifted my head from the knees of devotion where it lay. He eyed me askance and said,

Speak, brother, now
Amiably, cheerfully,
Before speech fails thee.
To-morrow thou
Silent perforce wilt be,
When grim Death hails thee.

One of my retainers informed him exactly how the case was: that I designed and had a fixed mind to pass the remnant of my days in sedulous piety, deeming silence the best society. "So," he continued, "take thine own road, if thou canst do it, and keep aloof or thou wilt rue it." "By the glory of God," cried he, "and by our long intimacy, I will not draw breath or flinch a single inch until he speaks to me in the familiar tone and the fashion well-known; for 'tis churlish to vex the heart of a friend, while a broken vow is easy to mend; and 'tis the judgment of fools and contrary to wisdom's rules that the sword of 'Alí rust in its sheath, or Sa'dí's tongue stick to his teeth.

Unless the tongue shall have turned
In the lock of the chamber of mind,
Whether jewels or trinkets behind
The door, by none is discerned.

Though 'Silence is good manners' teach the wise,
Try to speak when for speaking thou hast reason.
These are two marks of levity: to speak
At an ill time, and not speak in right season."

I thought it would be unkind to hold my tongue any more, and discourteous not to converse with him as before, since he was a congenial friend, and his love for me was unfeigned.

With him alone thy quarrel be,
Whom thou canst put to flight or flee.

We began talking and went a-walking. 'Twas spring-time: the traces of winter's ravage were no longer seen, and the rose had returned to be queen. As it fell out, I abode that night with one of my friends in a gay parterre, where a ceiling of tangled boughs quivered enchantingly in the cool air. It seemed as though on the sward pieces of coloured glass, small and fine, had been flung, and as though clusters of Pleiads on the vine had been hung. At dawn, when the inclination to go was prevailing over the wish to stay, I saw him towards the city bent, with a lapful of roses, hyacinth, basil, and other herbs of scent. "You know," said I, "that the rose will not endure, nor is the garden's promise sure; and sages have forbidden us to set our hearts on that which fades and departs." "What then?" said he. I replied, "To furnish the time present with reading merry and pleasant, I can compile the Book of the Rose-garden. Never shall autumn blast scatter its leaves away and the fury of October deform the loveliness of its May.

In vain thou fillest a vase with roses:
From my Rose-garden carry a leaf.
This blooms for ever, the reign of those is
Brief."

At once he let the flowers fall and caught the skirt of my robe and cried, "A gentleman keeps his word." That very day I jotted down a chapter on the social virtues and the customs of polite intercourse, in a style that will be useful to speakers and will increase the eloquence of letter-writers; and when I finished the book, there were still some roses left.

143

I saw an idol in the town Somnát[1],
Bejewelled, as in heathen days Manát[2],
And wrought of ivory with art extreme:
No fairer beauty couldst thou ever dream.
From every land come pilgrims to behold
And venerate that effigy unsouled;
From China and Chigil the rajahs flock,
Hoping true kindness from that heart of rock;
Before that image mute, and dumb withal,
The world's most eloquent, beseeching, fall.
In vain I asked myself, in vain explored,
Why living men a lifeless shape adored.

There was a Brahman who of me spoke well,
My friend and comrade, sharer of my cell.
Him softly I approached and sought his ear—
"Great is my wonder at the doings here:
How can a helpless idol so entrance
And hold them fast in bonds of ignorance?
No strength its hands, its feet no movement own,
It cannot rise up if you hurl it prone.
Its eyes are made of amber: 'tis unwise
To seek fidelity in stony eyes."
At this, my friend became my foe entire,
And he with anger blazed, and I caught fire.

[1] In Gujarát. The idol, which gives its name to the town, was destroyed by Sultan Maḥmúd of Ghazna in A.D. 1025.
[2] A goddess worshipped by the pagan Arabs.

He told the priests—in all the multitude
I did not see a face that promised good:
The pack of Guebres who Pá-Zand[1] intone
Set on me for the sake of that old bone[2].
Because the crook'd way straight and sure they deem,
The straight way crook'd accordingly must seem;
For though a man be wise and keen of wit,
He is a dunce where fools in judgment sit.
Lost as the drowning wretch, I saw no course
But to dissemble—'twas my one resource.
With savage enemy on vengeance bent,
The path to safety lies in soft consent.
Loud I extolled the Brahman archimage:
"O deep interpreter and master sage,
Me too this idol pleases with its grace
Of form and beauteous heart-bewitching face;
I find it marvellous in outward show,
But of the inward sense I nothing know.
I come to these parts late and have less skill,
A stranger, to distinguish good from ill.
But thou, who art as queen on this chessboard
And chief adviser of thy country's lord,
Thou know'st what meaning in this form may lie,
Of whose glad votaries the first am I.
To worship blindly is to go astray,
Happy the traveller that knows the way!"
The Brahman's visage gleamed with joy: on me
He looked approval. "Noble sir," said he,
"Thou hast done right to ask, and none dare chide:
They reach the journey's end who seek a guide.
Like thee, I have wandered much abroad; and ne'er
I saw an idol of itself aware,
Save this, which every morning from its stand
To God Almighty doth uplift a hand.

[1] Pázand, hyphenated above in order to indicate the pronunciation, refers here to the sacred books or litanies of the Hindus. The word is properly applied to an Avestic (Zend) transcription of a Pehlevi (Middle Persian) religious text.

[2] The ivory image.

If here thou wilt remain till night is gone,
Thou'lt see the mystery at to-morrow's dawn."
Here at the old man's bidding I remained,
Like Bízhan in the pit where he was chained[1].
Long as the Last Day seemed the night I stayed
Amidst the Guebres who unwashen prayed,
And priests unused to water: every one
Reeked as a carcase rotting in the sun.
Methought, I had committed some great sin,
The grievous torment so to linger in.
All night I lay with bosom sorrow-riven,
One hand pressed on my heart, one raised to heaven,
Till, hark, the drum's reveille in mine ear,
And voice of Brahman shrill as chanticleer!
Night, as a black-robed preacher risen to pray,
From willing scabbard drew the sword of Day;
The fire of Morning fell on cindery Night,
And in a moment all the world was bright.
As though mid negro swarms in Zanzibar
Stepped sudden forth a blue-eyed fair Tatár[2],
So eagerly, with unwashed faces, poured
From gate and court and street the miscreant horde.
Nor man nor woman in the town was left:
Not even a needle would have found a cleft
In that pagoda's throng. And there I stand,
Choking with grief, by slumber half unmanned—
When lo, the idol lifted up its hand!

At once from all a mighty shout arose,
Like to a raging sea when tempest blows.
Soon as the fane was emptied of its folk,
The Brahman, smiling, glanced at me and spoke:
"No longer, I perceive, art thou in doubt;
Falsehood is vanished, Truth shines clearly out."
Seeing him firm in ignorance and blind
To monstrous fancies rooted in his mind,
I durst not utter any word of sooth:
From falsehood's champions one must hide the truth.

[1] See p. 89 *supra*.
[2] The original spelling of "Tartar."

When thou behold'st an iron-fisted man,
To break thy fingers were a foolish plan.
I made pretence to weep, expressed my sore
Contrition for the words I spake before.
Tears moved their miscreant hearts, and at the shock
They yielded, as the torrent moves the rock;
Toward me with low obeisance then they sped
And took my arm and to the idol led.
I sued for pardon to that ivory form
In chair of gold on ebon throne enorm;
I kissed the despicable idol's hand—
Accurst be it, accurst the adoring band!
For some while I the infidels did ape
And learned the priestly doctrine's every shape.
At length they trusted me within the fane;
So glad was I, scarce Earth could me contain.
I bolted fast the temple-door one night,
And darting like a scorpion left and right,
Looked up and down, the ebon throne beside,
Until a gold-embroidered screen I spied:
Behind it sat the attendant devotee,
And in his hand an end of cord had he!
The riddle was resolved, and plain the tracks
As when for David iron grew as wax[1].
At once I saw that when he pulls the cord,
The idol's hand is lifted to its Lord.
Ashamed to meet mine eye, the priest devout—
His foul disgrace thus turned all inside out—
Started to run, and after him I flew:
The rascal headlong down a well I threw;
For 'twas most certain he would ever strive
To murder me, if he remained alive,
And fearing lest his secret I betray,
Would not be loth to strike my life away[2].
I slew the villain with a stone outright,
For dead men tell no tales; then took to flight.

[1] God taught David the art of making coats of mail (Koran, XXI, 80).

[2] Here I have omitted three verses on the folly of sparing a dangerous enemy when it is in your power to despatch him.

144

Until thine hands clasp girdlewise the waist of the Belov'd,
Thou ne'er wilt kiss to heart's desire the mouth of the Belov'd.
Know'st thou what is the life of him the sword of Love hath
slain?
To bite an apple from the orchard-cheek of the Belov'd.
Khusrau and Shírín's mighty love is rased and washed away
By tide of turmoil swelling high 'twixt me and the Belov'd.
The champion whom in far war's field no paynim arrow slew,
His blood was shed by bow-like fair eyebrow of the Belov'd.
Gone is mine heart, mine eye weeps blood; and if my faint
soul lives,
'Tis only that I may bestow its life on the Belov'd.
Ay, one day I will fling myself beneath his Arab's hoof,
Unless disdain and pride pull in the rein of the Belov'd.
Howbeit in this quest, alas, I never win to joy,
It may be that my name will pass the lips of the Belov'd.
Sith life must once be yielded up, whatever fate befall,
Most sweet to die in Love's abode at the door of the Belov'd!
Surely will I then bear with me this passion to the grave,
And from the grave arise and ask the way to the Belov'd.
All men cry out against the hand of hated enemy,
But Sa'dí cries against the unloving heart of the Belov'd.

145

Dear to me this lamentation, though it melt my soul with fire,
For it passes the day somehow: surely else I should expire.
Not so beautiful is Morning, setting earth and heaven alight,
As the face for which I waited, waited all this weary night.
Ah, if I may see again that love-enkindling face, now far,
Thanks I'll say till Resurrection unto my victorious star.
If I shrink when blame is cast on me, I play the woman's part:
Howsoe'er the arrow pierce thee, meet it with a manly heart!
They that hunger after pleasure needs must know the taste
of pain:
He that hopes for New Year's springtide, let him freeze and
not complain!

Prudent harvesters of reason love's deep bliss did never learn:
'Tis Majnún reads Lailà's secret—he whose wits in frenzy burn.
Fling thy noose about another! Self-devoted here I stand:
Who would tie the foot of falcon long familiar with his hand?
Lovers gambling all the goods away of that world and of this
Are endowed with something precious that our sleek ascetics miss.
Yesterday is gone, To-morrow not yet come. Do thou waylay
Opportunity, O Sa'dí! Make the utmost of To-day!

146

Lovers' souls 'gin dance with glee
When the zephyr fans thy roses.
Ne'er melts thy stony heart for me,
Mine as a sunk stone heavily
In thy dimple's well reposes.

Life were an offering too small,
Else 'tis easy to surrender
Unto thee, who need'st not call
Painter's art to deck thy wall:
Thou alone dost give it splendour.

Better sicken, better die
At thy feet than live to lose thee.
Pilgrim to Love's sanctuary,
What car'st thou, 'neath desert sky,
How the thorns of Absence bruise thee?

147

The heart that loves with patience—a stone 'tis, not a heart;
Nay, love and patience dwell of old a thousand leagues apart.
O brethren of the mystic path, leave blame and me alone!
Repentance in the way of Love is glass against a stone.
No more in secret need I drink, in secret dance and sing:
For us that love religiously, good name's a shameful thing.
What right and justice should I see or what instruction hear?
Mine eye is to the Sáḳí[1] turned, and to the lute mine ear.

[1] The cupbearer.

I caught the zephyr's fluttering skirt for sweet remembrance' sake:
Alas, I have ta'en but empty wind where scent I hoped to take.
Who'll bring a message to my Dear that off in anger went?
Go, tell him I have dropped the shield, if he on war is bent;
And let him kill as he knows how! for if no vision there be
Of him, the wide world seems a cramped uneasy place to me.

148

O cameleer, drive gently now! My soul's delight is fain to flee,
And takes away with her the heart which I before kept safe with me.
Here I remain unblest by her, despairing and distressed by her;
Methinks, a lancet pressed by her doth pierce my bones, tho' far she be.
"With many a charm and spell," I cried, "this inward ulcer I will hide":
Lo, streaming o'er the lintel wide my blood lets out the mystery.
My Friend departed in disdain and left me to a life of pain,
Dark fumes are mounting from my brain: like coals of fire I burn, ah me!
With all her cruelty and scorn, her pledges vain and vows forsworn,
Still on my tongue her name is borne, and in my breast her memory.
Hold back the howdahs, camel-man! Chide not the tardy caravan!
I soar beyond mine earthly span for love of that fair cypress-tree.

ABU 'L-BAḲÁ OF RONDA

THE author of this affecting poem was a Spanish Arab, who probably wrote it *circa* A.D. 1250, after the collapse of the Moorish empire in Spain. Seville was captured by Ferdinand III in A.D. 1248.

149

Spain hath been stricken by a calamity for which there is no consolation; because of it Uḥud is fallen and Thahlán lies in ruins[1].
The evil eye hath smitten her Islam, and so deeply hath she been afflicted that in many provinces and towns not a Moslem is left.
Ask Valencia what is the plight of Murcia! And where now is Xativa or where is Jaen?
And where is Cordova, the home of learning, in which many a great scholar rose to renown?
And where is Seville with all her delights and her sweet river whose waters are full and overflowing?—
Noble cities that were the pillars of the land; and how can the land subsist when the pillars are no more?
As a fond lover weeps at parting from his beloved, bitterly weeps the glorious religion of Abraham[2]
For desolate countries forsaken by Islam and peopled only by infidelity.
Their mosques have become churches: there is nothing in them but bells[3] and crosses,
So that the *miḥrábs* (niches) weep, though lifeless, and the *minbars* (pulpits) mourn, though wooden.
O thou that heedest not the warning of Fortune—if thou art asleep, yet is Fortune awake!
O thou that walkest jubilantly, charmed by thy place of abode—is any man beguiled by a fair abode after the loss of Seville?
That disaster made us forget those preceding it, and for all the length of time it will never be forgotten.
O ye that ride noble horses, slender and swift as eagles on the field of honour,

[1] Uḥud is the name of a mountain near Medina; Thahlán, of a mountain in Najd (Central Arabia). By this hyperbole the poet indicates the shattering effect of the disaster.

[2] Islam. Mohammed declared that he was sent to preach the true religion of Abraham, which succeeding generations had corrupted.

[3] The *náḳús* was originally a clapper of wood, such as is used by Christians in the East for calling to prayer.

And bear keen-edged Indian swords gleaming like fires amidst dark clouds of dust,
And chew the cud of ease, powerful and glorious in your homes beyond the sea[1],
Have ye no word of the people of Spain?—yet all night have riders carried their news to you.
How long will the sons of the despised, who are slain and captive, cry for succour and not a man of you be roused?
Why this estrangement between Moslems? O servants of Alláh, ye all are brothers!
Are there no proud souls, generous and of high courage? Is there none to aid and champion the good cause?
Oh, who will come to the help of a people once mighty but now abased, once flourishing but now oppressed by unbelievers?
Yesterday they were kings in their dwelling-places, and to-day they are slaves in the land of the infidel.
And what if thou couldst see them stricken with consternation, with none to guide them, wearing the garments of ignominy!
Couldst thou but see them weeping when they are sold, the sight would dismay thee and throw thee into a frenzy of grief.
Ah, betwixt many a mother and child comes such a sundering as when souls are parted from bodies!
And many a young girl beauteous as the new-risen sun, blushing like rubies and coral,
The barbarian drags to shame by force, her eyes weeping, her mind distraught.
A sight like this melts the heart with anguish, if in the heart there be a Moslem's feeling and faith.

*Ḥáfiẓ

150

Sáḳí, pass the cup and pour,
Pour me out the balmy drink!
Love, who seemed so light of yore,
Underneath his load I sink.

[1] The poet appeals to the Almohades in North Africa to come to the help of their Moslem kinsfolk.

Quoth mine ancient Guide, who knows
Every inn upon the way:
"Well for you if purple flows
O'er the carpet as ye pray!"

Zephyr, quick! blow loose the knot
Of my Sweetheart's tangled hair!
'Tis the heart of all the plot
Laid against my life, I swear.

Sea and storm and dead of night,
Midst the whirlpool's ghastly roar:
Ah, what know they of our plight,
Happy loiterers on the shore?

In this mansion of Farewell
Pleasure, ere it comes, is gone,
Where a never silent bell
Tolls "Arise and journey on!"

Hafiz, tired of blame and praise,
If thy spirit longs for rest,
Leave the world and all its ways,
Clasp the Loved One to thy breast!

151

The writing on the pages of the Rose
(For readers all are not interpreters)
Only the Nightingale may understand.

I murmured to my soul apart: "Suppose
Thy throne o'ercanopied the universe—"
"Love, love endures; the rest is crumbling sand."

O Love, in search of thee whoever goes
To Reason's school, goes farther and fares worse:
For him no face-to-face or hand-in-hand!

152

Love's hidden pearl is shining yet,
And Love's sealed casket bears the same device
As it bore of old;
The tears with which mine eyes are wet
Roll, as yesterday they rolled,

Roll, as they shall roll to-morrow,
Fraught with blood of sacrifice,
From the same fountain of eternal sorrow.

Ah, could my heart but speak
Or thou divine
What passion-flower is this
That lent its colour to those lips of thine!
What ruby blushes o'er thy lovely cheek,
Dreaming of the sun's hot kiss
In the darkness of the mine!
Ah, could my heart but speak
Or thou divine!

153

My soul is the veil of his love,
Mine eye is the glass of his grace.
Not for earth, not for heaven above,
Would I stoop; yet his bounties have bowed
A spirit too proud
For aught to abase.

This temple of awe, where no sin
But only the zephyr comes nigh,
Who am I to adventure within?
Even so: very foul is my skirt.
What then? Will it hurt
The most Pure, the most High?

He passed by the rose in the field,
His colour and perfume she stole.
O twice happy star that revealed
The secret of day and of night—
His face to my sight,
His love to my soul!

154

Fetch me wine! for the Fast-month is o'er,
Name and fame are in season no more.
Dost thou hear? On this bench soon and late
For a drop of thy liquor I wait.

Too long I have burned in the fire
Of repentance and barren desire.
O the smell of the grape!—Jesu's breath
To my soul—it revives me from death.

Let me drink, let me haste to make up
Precious time spent away from the cup,
Drink till Fancy knows nothing about
What comes into her head or goes out!

Proud monk, spare me homilies, pray!
I from virtue am far, far astray.
Yes; but Heav'n to which thou hast no key
Opens wide to poor sinners like me.

155

Mortal never won to view thee,
Yet a thousand lovers woo thee;
Not a nightingale but knows
In the rosebud sleeps the rose.

Love is where the glory falls
Of thy face: on convent walls
Or on tavern floors the same
Unextinguishable flame.

Where the turban'd anchorite
Chanteth Allah day and night,
Churchbells ring the call to prayer,
And the Cross of Christ is there.

156

O Beauty worshipped ever
With what sweet pain and joy,
Hid from the world's endeavour,
But seen by spirit's eye!

Alike in mosque and tavern
Thou art my only thought;
The hermit in his cavern,
He seeks what I have sought.

Belov'd, unveil the splendour
Of all the skies and spheres—
Let thy moon-face so tender
Swim through my starry tears!

157

The calm circumference of life
When I would fain have kept,
Time caught me in the tide of strife
And to the centre swept.

Of this fierce glow which Love and You
Within my breast inspire,
The Sun is but a spark that flew
And set the heavens afire!

158

Blame not us wild rogues and gay,
As if *our* score *thou* must pay.
Saint or sinner, every one
Reaps at last what he hath sown.
Am I given to wine or prayer?
Pardon, that is my affair.
If I from virtue fell to vice,
My father lost a Paradise.
Thou who bidd'st me hopeless be
Of God's predestined charity,
Dost thou know behind the Veil
Who laughs in bliss, who weeps in bale?
Drunk or dry, the world entire
Hath one Object of desire.
Whether to mosque or church we come,
Love is everywhere at home.
On the tavern's lintel now
Resteth my devoted brow.
Kneel thou too, O critic dull,
And knock some wits into thy skull!
Cup in hand let Hafiz die,
Straight to Eden he will fly!

159

'Twas the birthday of the world this famous carouse began.
Devotion, piety, faith! and I so richly decayed!
Tho' Love's strong wine hath wasted and left me a broken man,
I build immortal life on the ruin that Love hath made.

Washed in the fountain of Love, that moment I took farewell,
Farewell for ever, of earth and sky and the sum of things.
Fill me a cup once more! Fate's mystery I will tell,
Whose face enravished my soul, whose scent gave my spirit wings.

160

Wise men! beware of dealing
In Life's vast house of trade;
'Tis packed, from floor to ceiling,
With goods of Nothing made.

Come, while on shore we linger,
O Sáḳí, let not slip
An hour of Time whose finger
Points out to yon dark ship.

Laugh like the rose! What matter,
This month of fragrant eves,
Tho' autumn's blast shall scatter
Our unregarded leaves?

A Paradise of pleasure
Bought with a world of pain—
Fie on the luckless treasure
That I must bleed to gain!

161

Birds are piping on the boughs, the Zephyr blows a valentine
To the Vintner, "Luck, old fellow! may you soon have sold your wine!"
Listen, for to me this morning whispered low a heavenly voice,
"'Tis the season of enjoyment: come, make merry and rejoice!"

What, I wonder, to the Lily said the lovelorn Nightingale,
That with all her golden tongues she cannot tell the mystic tale?
We jolly brethren of the grape let none profane our feast;
Sáḳí, cover up the flagon! Here he comes, the canting priest.
I will sing you songs again and you will wreathe my head,
But stay, good Angel, stay till cursèd Ahriman be fled.
Cloister, fare thee well! The Tavern calls me—there will I reside,
Washing down with honest liquor fumes of cant and airs of pride.

162

Pure wine and fair women
Are pits on the way,
To inveigle the wisest
Who are moulded of clay.

Am I a wild lover,
A black-listed sot?
My friends in the city
Bear names without spot.

Oh, enter devoutly
The tavern! This ring
Of topers that haunt it
Have ear of the King.

Despise not the dervish
Whose throne is the ground,
The emperor swordless,
The monarch uncrowned!

Beware! When high bloweth
The wind of disdain,
Whole stacks of obeisance
Are worth not a grain.

163

Till the scent of wine is forgot and the tavern buries its sign,
I fling me in headlong worship before the Maker of wine.

I have served Him ere the beginning of Time that never began,
I shall serve Him ages and ages beyond the vision of man.
Pass not my tomb so proudly! A blessing waits on thy prayer,
For the whole generation of topers will flock to pilgrimage there.
Bitter they call thee, child of the grape, and load thee with shames,
But to me thou art sweeter than kisses, thy name is the sweetest of names.
One, perhaps, with a scrupulous beard hath Folly to wife;
'Tis we bacchanalian sinners unlock the magic of life.
Happy, thrice happy, who cannot tell at loving-cup's close,
Whether head on the threshold or whether turban he throws!
I knocked at Virtue's gate, but they drove me away in scorn.
Is Hafiz to blame, or the ruling star when Hafiz was born?

Ibn Khaldún

Ibn Khaldún, the great philosophical historian, was born in A.D. 1332 at Tunis and died, as Cadi of Cairo, in A.D. 1406. He stood far in advance of his age, and we must look for his successors not in the Moslem world but in medieval and modern Europe. Although the style of the *Muḳaddama* (Prolegomena) is somewhat cumbrous and involved, the immense range of the author's knowledge, the originality of his ideas, and his masterly treatment of the subject render his work indispensable to students of Islamic civilisation.

164

Prolegomena showing the excellence of the science of History, establishing the methods proper to it, and glancing at the errors into which Historians fall, together with some account of their causes.

Know that the science of History is noble in its conception, abounding in instruction, and exalted in its aim. It acquaints us with the characteristics of the ancient peoples, the ways of life followed by the prophets, and the dynasties and government of kings, so that those who wish may draw valuable lessons for their guidance in religious and worldly affairs.

The student of History, however, requires numerous sources of information and a great variety of knowledge; he must consider well and examine carefully in order to arrive at the truth and avoid errors and pitfalls. If he rely on bare tradition, without having thoroughly grasped the principles of common experience, the institutes of government, the nature of civilisation, and the circumstances of human society, and without judging what is past and invisible by the light of what is present before his eyes, then he will often be in danger of stumbling and slipping and losing the right road. Many errors committed by historians, commentators, and leading traditionists in their narrative of events have been caused by their reliance on mere tradition, which they have accepted without regard to its (intrinsic) worth, neglecting to refer it to its general principles, judge it by its analogies, and test it by the standard of wisdom, knowledge of the natures of things, and exact historical criticism. Thus they have gone astray from the truth and wandered in the desert of imagination and error. Especially is this the case in computing sums of money and numbers of troops, when such matters occur in their narratives; for here falsehood and exaggeration are to be expected, and one must always refer to general principles and submit to the rules (of probability). For example, Mas'údí and many other historians relate that Moses—on whom be peace!—numbered the armies of the Israelites in the wilderness, after he had reviewed all the men capable of bearing arms who were twenty years old or above that age, and that they amounted to 600,000 or more. Now, in making this statement he forgot to consider whether Egypt and Syria are large enough to support armies of that size, for it is a fact attested by well-known custom and familiar experience that every kingdom keeps for its defence only such a force as it can maintain and furnish with rations and pay. Moreover, it would be impossible for armies so huge to march against each other or fight, because the territory is too limited in extent to allow of it, and because, when drawn up in ranks, they would cover a space twice or three times as far as the eye can reach, if not more. How should these two hosts engage in battle, or one of them gain the victory, when neither wing knows anything of what is happening on the other? The present time bears witness to the truth of my observations: water is not so like to water as the future to the past.

The Persian Empire was much greater than the kingdom of the Israelites, as appears from the conquest of the latter by Nebuchadnezzar, who attacked their country, made himself master of their dominions, and laid waste Jerusalem, the chief seat of their religion and power, although he was only the governor of a Persian province: it is said that he was the satrap of the western frontiers. The Persians ruled over the two 'Iráḳs, Khurásán, Transoxania, and the lands opening on the Caspian Sea—an empire far more extensive than that of the Israelites; yet their armies never equalled or even approached the number mentioned above. Their army at Ḳádisíya, the greatest they ever mustered, was 120,000 strong, and each of these was accompanied by a retainer. Saif, by whom this is related, adds that the whole force exceeded 200,000. According to 'Á'isha and Zuhrí, the troops under Rustam who were opposed to Sa'd at Ḳádisíya were only 60,000 strong, each man having a follower.

Again, if the Israelites had reached this total, vast would have been the extent of their kingdom and wide the range of their power. Provinces and kingdoms are small or great in proportion to the numbers of their soldiery and population, as we shall explain in the chapter concerning empires in the First Book. Now, it is well-known that the territories of the Israelites did not extend, in Syria, beyond al-Urdunn and Palestine, and in the Ḥijáz, beyond the districts of Yathrib (Medina) and Khaibar.

Furthermore, according to the trustworthy authorities, there were only four fathers (generations) between Moses and Israel. Moses was the son of 'Imrán the son of Yas-hur the son of Káhat or Káhit the son of Láwí or Láwá the son of Jacob or Isrá'ílu 'llah (Israel of God). This is his genealogy as given in the Pentateuch. The length of time separating them is recorded by Mas'údí, who says that when Israel entered Egypt and came to Joseph with his sons, the (twelve) Patriarchs and their children, seventy persons in all, they abode in Egypt under the dominion of the Pharaohs, the kings of the Copts, two hundred and twenty years until they went forth into the wilderness with Moses, on whom be peace. It is incredible that in the course of four generations their offspring should have multiplied so enormously.

165

That being so, the rule for distinguishing the true from the false in history is based on possibility or impossibility; that is to say, we must examine human society, by which I mean civilisation, and discriminate between the characteristics essential to it and inherent in its nature and those which are accidental and unimportant, recognising further those which cannot possibly belong to it. If we do that, we shall have a canon for separating historical fact and truth from error and falsehood by a method of proof that admits of no doubt; and then, if we hear an account of any of the things that happen in civilised society, we shall know how to distinguish what we judge to be worthy of acceptance from what we judge to be spurious, having in our hands an infallible criterion which enables historians to verify whatever they relate.

Such is the purpose of the First Book of the present work. And it would seem that this is an independent science. For it has a subject, namely, human civilisation and society; and problems, namely, to explain in succession the accidental features and essential characters of civilisation. This is the case with every science, the intellectual as well as those founded on authority.

The matter of the following discourse is novel, original, and instructive. I have discovered it by dint of deep thought and research. It appertains not to the science of oratory, which is only concerned with such language as will convince the multitude and be useful for winning them over to an opinion or persuading them to reject the same. Nor, again, does it form part of the science of civil government, *i.e.* the proper regulation of a household or city in accordance with moral and philosophical laws, in order that the people may be led to live in a way that tends to preserve and perpetuate the species. These two sciences may resemble it, but its subject differs from theirs. It appears to be a new invention; and indeed I have not met with a discourse upon it by any one in the world. I do not know whether this is due to their neglect of the topic—and we need not think the worse of them for that—or whether, perhaps, they may have treated it exhaustively in books that have not come down to us. Amongst the races of mankind the sciences are many and the savants numerous, and the knowledge we have lost is greater in amount than all that has reached us. What has become of the sciences of the Persians, whose writings were destroyed by 'Umar (may God be well-pleased with him!) at the time of the conquest? Where are those of Chaldaea, Assyria, and Babylonia, with all that they produced and left behind them? Where are those of the Copts and of peoples yet more ancient? We have received the sciences of but one nation, the Greeks, and that only because Ma'mún took pains to have their books translated from the language in which they were composed. He was enabled to do this by finding plenty of translators and expending large sums on the work. Of the sciences of other peoples we know nothing.

* * * * *

Now we shall set forth in this Book the various features of civilisation as they appear in human society: kingship, acquisition of wealth, the sciences, and the arts. We shall employ demonstrative methods to verify and elucidate the knowledge spread amongst all classes, to refute false opinions, and to remove uncertainties.

Man is distinguished from the other animals by attributes peculiar to himself. Amongst these are

(1) The sciences and arts produced by the faculty of reflection, which distinguishes men from the animals and exalts him above the rest of created beings.

(2) The need for an authority to restrain and a government to coerce him. Of the animals he is the only one that cannot exist without this. As for what is said concerning bees and locusts, even if they have something of the sort,

they have it by instinct, not from reflection and consideration.

(3) The labour and industry which supply him with diverse ways and means of obtaining a livelihood, inasmuch as God has made nourishment necessary to him for the maintenance of his life and has directed him to seek it and search after it. "*He gave unto all things their nature: then He directed*[1]."

(4) Civilisation, *i.e.* settling down and dwelling together in a city or in tents for the sake of social intercourse and for the satisfaction of their needs, because men are naturally disposed to help each other to subsist, as we shall explain presently. This civilisation is either nomadic (*badawí*) or residential (*ḥaḍarí*). The former is found in steppes and mountains, among the pastoral tribes of the desert and the inhabitants of remote sands; the latter in towns, villages, cities, and cultivated tracts, whither men resort for safety and in order to be protected by walls. In all these circumstances it exhibits the phenomena characteristic of a social state. Accordingly, the matter of this Book must be comprised in six chapters:

I. Human society in general, its various divisions, and the part of the earth which it occupies.
II. Nomadic civilisation, with an account of the wild tribes and peoples.
III. Dynasties, the Caliphate, kingship, and the high offices of government.
IV. The settled civilisation of countries and cities.
V. Crafts, means of livelihood, and the various ways of making money.
VI. The sciences, and how they are acquired and learned.

166

The tribes of the desert are kept off from each other by the authority of their chiefs and elders, whom they respect greatly. For the defence of their encampments against a foreign enemy, each tribe has a troop of warriors and knights

[1] Koran, XX, 52.

famous for their prowess; but they would not make a firm resistance and defence unless they were united by kinship and a feeling of solidarity (*'aṣabíya*). That is what renders them so strong and formidable. *Esprit de corps* and devotion to one's kin is of supreme importance. The affection which God has put in the hearts of His servants towards those of their own flesh and blood is inherent in human nature: it leads them to help and succour one another and inspires their foes with terror. The Koran gives an example in the story of the brothers of Joseph (on whom be peace!), when they said to their father, "*If the wolf devour him, when we are banded together* (*for his protection*), *we shall be weaklings indeed*[1]," *i.e.*, it is inconceivable that violence should be done to any one so long as he has devoted partisans. In those who are not drawn together by the bonds of kinship this feeling towards their comrades is seldom aroused: when dark war-clouds threaten disaster, every man will slip away in alarm to look after his own safety, because he fears to be forsaken by his allies. Such a people cannot live in the desert: they would fall an easy prey to any race that attacked them. Now, if this is clear with regard to those dwelling together, who must needs defend and protect themselves, similarly you will see that it holds good in the case of any enterprise that excites hostility, such as the mission of a prophet or the founding of a kingdom or the propaganda of a sect. An object of this kind is only attained by fighting for it, since opposition is natural to man; and in order to fight with success, there must be a feeling of solidarity as we said just now. Let this principle be your guide in perusing the observations which we are about to make. God aids us to arrive at the truth.

167

On the inability of the Arabs to establish an empire unless they are imbued with religion by a prophet or a saint, or generally inspired by religious enthusiasm.

The reason of this is that, being naturally wild, they are of all peoples the most reluctant to submit to one another

[1] Koran, XII, 14.

owing to the rudeness of their manners, their arrogance, their high spirit, and their jealousy of authority. Seldom, therefore, are they unanimous. But when they follow a prophet or a saint, they are restrained by something within themselves; their pride and jealousy depart from them, submission and concord are no longer difficult. Religion brings them together: it takes away their rudeness and insolence, it removes envy and jealousy from their hearts. If there be among them the prophet or saint who urges them to fulfil the command of God, and requires that they shall abandon their evil ways and cleave to the good, and bids them be of one voice to make the truth prevail, they will become completely united and gain victory and empire. Moreover, no people is so quick to receive the truth and the right. Their natures are uncorrupted by vicious habits and free from base qualities; and as for their savagery, it is conformable and adaptable to good in consequence of its having preserved the original constitution of man (which renders him capable of accepting the true religion), and because it is remote from the bad habits and dispositions which stamp themselves on men's souls. For, according to the Apostolic Tradition already quoted, "Every one is born with a capacity for receiving the truth."

168

Showing that empires, like individuals, have their natural term of life

You must know that physicians and astrologers declare the natural life of man to be a hundred and twenty years of the kind which astrologers call "the greatest years of the moon"; but it varies in every race according to the conjunctions of the planets, so that sometimes it is more than this and sometimes less. Those born under certain planetary conjunctions live a full century, others fifty years or seventy or eighty; and stargazers believe that all this is indicated by the position of the heavenly bodies. In the Moslem community, as is recorded in Traditions of the Prophet, life runs to sixty or seventy years. The natural life, *i.e.* 120 years, is rarely exceeded: such cases as that of Noah (on whom be peace!), and a few of the people of 'Ád and Thamúd, depend on extraordinary positions in the celestial sphere. The lives of empires, too, vary according to the conjunctions of the planets; but as a rule an empire does not last more than three generations—reckoning a generation as the middle life of an individual, *i.e.* 40 years, a period which marks the end of the body's growth and development: God has said, "*Until, when he reaches his age of strength and attains unto forty years....*[1]" For this reason we said that the length of a generation is the (middle) life of an individual. Our statement is confirmed by what we have already mentioned touching the Divine wisdom which decreed that the Israelites should pass forty years in the wilderness, and the purpose thereof, namely, that the generation then living might decease and another grow up, which had never known the abasement (of slavery). That indicates that forty years, which is the (middle) life of an individual, is the length of a generation.

An empire, as we remarked, seldom outlives three generations. The first maintains its nomadic character, its rude and savage ways of life; inured to hardships, brave, fierce, and sharing renown with each other, the tribesmen preserve their solidarity in full vigour: their swords are kept sharp, their attack is feared, and their neighbours vanquished. With the second generation comes a change. Possessing dominion and affluence, they turn from nomadic to settled life, and from hardship to ease and plenty. The authority, instead of being shared by all, is appropriated by one, while the rest, too spiritless to make an effort to regain it, abandon the glory of ambition for the shame of subjection. Their solidarity is weakened in some degree; yet one may notice that notwithstanding the indignity to which they submit, they retain much of what they have known and witnessed in the former generation—the feelings of fierceness and pride, the desire for honour, and the resolution to defend themselves and repulse their foes. These qualities they cannot lose entirely, though a part be gone. They hope to become again such men as their fathers were, or they fancy that the old virtues still survive amongst them.

[1] Koran, XLVI, 14.

In the third generation the wandering life and rough manners of the desert are forgotten, as though they had never been. At this stage men no longer take delight in glory and patriotism, since all have learned to bow under the might of a sovereign and are so addicted to luxurious pleasures that they have become a burden on the state; for they require protection like the women and young boys. Their national spirit is wholly extinguished; they have no stomach for resistance, defence, or attack. Nevertheless they impose on the people by their (military) appearance and uniform, their horsemanship, and the address with which they manœuvre. It is but a false show: they are in general greater cowards than the most helpless women, and will give way at the first assault. The monarch in those days must needs rely on the bravery of others, enrol many of the clients (freedmen), and recruit soldiers capable, to some extent, of guarding the empire, until God proclaims the hour of its destruction and it falls with everything that it upholds. Thus do empires age and decay in the course of three generations.

*JÁMÍ

NÚRU'DDÍN 'ABDU 'R-RAḤMÁN JÁMÍ (A.D. 1414–1492) was, in the words used by Professor Browne (*Persian Literature under Tartar Dominion*, p. 507) "one of the most remarkable geniuses whom Persia ever produced, for he was at once a great poet, a great scholar, and a great mystic." The best apology I can make for the few brief extracts given below is the hope that they will cause the reader to seek full satisfaction in the book from which I have quoted.

169

The Creation of the World

From all eternity the Beloved unveiled His beauty in the solitude of the Unseen;
He held up the mirror to His own face, He displayed His loveliness to Himself.
He was both the spectator and the spectacle; no eye but His had surveyed the universe.

All was One, there was no duality, no pretence of 'mine' or 'thine.'
The vast orb of Heaven, with its myriad incomings and outgoings, was concealed in a single point.
The Creation lay cradled in the sleep of non-existence, like a child ere it has breathed.
The eye of the Beloved, seeing what was not, regarded nonentity as existent.
Although he beheld His attributes and qualities as a perfect whole in His own essence,
Yet He desired that they should be displayed to Him in another mirror,
And that each one of His eternal attributes should become manifest accordingly in a diverse form.
Therefore He created the verdant fields of Time and Space and the life-giving garden of the world,
That every bough and leaf and fruit might show forth His various perfections.
The cypress gave a hint of His comely stature, the rose gave tidings of His beauteous countenance.
Wherever Beauty peeped out, Love appeared beside it; wherever Beauty shone in a rosy cheek, Love lit his torch from that flame.
Wherever Beauty dwelt in dark tresses, Love came and found a heart entangled in their coils.
Beauty and Love are as body and soul; Beauty is the mine and Love the precious stone.
They have always been together from the very first: never have they travelled but in each other's company.

170

Manṣúr Ḥalláj was asked, "Who is the true lover of God?" He replied, "The true lover of God is he that rests in naught, and bestows on none other a thought, from the moment when he sets forth to seek until he hath found what he sought."

Swift for Thy sake I sped o'er land and sea,
And clove a way through wold and steep, heart-free,
And turned aside from all I met, until
I found the shrine where I am one with Thee.

171

Shiblí—God sanctify his spirit!—fell into a frenzy. He was brought to the mad-house, and a number of his friends came to see him. "Who are ye?" he asked. They said, "We are thy friends." He picked up a stone and rushed at them. They all fled. "Come back," he shouted, "hypocrites as ye are! Friends from friends take not flight or shun the stones of their despite."

He is thy friend who, wronged by thee his friend,
The more thou harm'st him loveth thee the more;
Whom thou mayst pelt with stones and only make
His love's foundation firmer than before.

172

"What is Ṣúfism?" they asked Shaikh Abú Sa'íd son of Abu 'l-Khair. He answered: "Put away all thou hast in thy head, give all thou hast in thy hand, and do not shrink from whatsoever befalls thee."

Wouldst thou thyself from selfhood disembroil,
To banish vain desire must be thy toil,
Empty thy hand of all it closes on,
And suffer many a blow and not recoil.

173

The Emperor Núshírwán was holding an assembly on the day of Naurúz[1] or Mihrján[2] when he saw one of the guests, who was a kinsman of his, lift a golden cup and hide it under his arm. He feigned not to see and said nothing. When the assembly was about to break up, the wine-server exclaimed, "Let none depart till I make search. A golden cup is missing." "No matter," said Núshírwán, "for he who took it will not give it back, and he who saw it taken will not tell." Some days afterwards that person came to Núshírwán in new clothes and new boots. Núshírwán pointed to his clothes as though to say, "I know what bought these." The other raised his skirt and showed his boots, as if he would add, "And these

[1] The spring festival.   [2] The autumn festival.

too." Núshírwán laughed, for he perceived that need and want had caused his kinsman to steal the cup; and he bestowed on him a thousand pieces of gold.

When thy offence to gracious king is known,
Avow it and beseech him to condone.
Deny it not! Else thou committ'st, beside,
A second fault much worse than that denied.

174

Jáḥiẓ[1] said: "I never felt so ashamed of myself as one day when a woman laid hold of me and led me to a brassfounder's shop and said to the master, 'Like this!' I was at a loss and begged him to explain. 'She bade me make for her an image of the Devil,' he replied; 'and when I told her that I did not know what it should be like, she fetched you as the model.'"

175

It is related that one day in the presence of the Sultan of the mystic Path, Shaikh Abú Sa'íd—may God sanctify his spirit!—a *ḳawwál* chanted this verse:

"I'll hide myself within my song of love,
That I may kiss thee when thou singest it."

The Shaikh was delighted. "Who is the poet?" he asked. "'Umára," they replied. "Come," said he to his disciples, "let us pay him a visit"; and he set off, accompanied by them all.

[1] See p. 47 *supra*. Jáḥiẓ was notorious for his ugliness.

APPENDIX

As some readers of these translations may wish to consult the original passages either for the purpose of comparison or for any other reason, I give here a numbered list indicating the source of the English version in each case. *Ḥamâsa* refers to the edition of Freytag with Tibrízí's commentary (Bonn, 1828); *Delectus* to Th. Nöldeke's *Delectus veterum carminum Arabicorum* (Berlin, 1890).

1. *Ḥamâsa*, 423, 11. *Delectus*, 41, 3.
2. *Ḥamâsa*, 9, 17. *Delectus*, 45, 10.
3. *Ḥamâsa*, 252, 14. *Delectus*, 46, 16.
4. *Delectus*, 44, 7.
5. The *Mu'allaḳa* of Imra'u 'l-Ḳais, in *Septem Mo'allaḳât*, ed. by F. A. Arnold (Leipzig, 1850), pp. 11–16, vv. 23–35.
6. *Le Diwan d'Amro'lkais*, ed. by Baron MacGuckin de Slane (Paris, 1837), p. 25, v. 16 to p. 26, v. 12. *The Divans of the six ancient Arabic poets*, ed. by W. Ahlwardt (London, 1870), pp. 128–9, vv. 1–17.
7. *Ibid.* p. 22, vv. 7–19. *The Divans*, ed. by W. Ahlwardt, p. 154, vv. 47–59.
8. The *Mu'allaḳa* of Ṭarafa in *A commentary on ten ancient Arabic poems*, ed. by Sir C. J. Lyall (Calcutta, 1894), p. 43, vv. 54–59; *Septem Mo'allaḳât*, ed. by Arnold, pp. 54–56, vv. 56–61.
9. The *Mu'allaḳa* of 'Amr ibn Kulthúm in *Septem Mo'allaḳât*, ed. by Arnold, pp. 120–1, vv. 1–8; pp. 125–7, vv. 19–30; pp. 133–4, vv. 54–59; pp. 142–4, vv. 94–104, omitting 100, 101; and in *A commentary on ten ancient Arabic poems*, ed. by Sir C. J. Lyall, pp. 108–10, vv. 1–7; pp. 111–12, vv. 15–18; pp. 112–14, vv. 20–30, omitting 22, 27, 28; pp. 117–18, vv. 46–51, omitting 48; pp. 121–2, vv. 75–79; pp. 123–4, vv. 91–95, omitting 92.
10. The *Mu'allaḳa* of Zuhair in *Septem Mo'allaḳât*, pp. 74–5, vv. 16–19; pp. 78–9, vv. 27–31; pp. 85–7, vv. 47, 49, 48, 50, 52, 51, 57, 54; and in Lyall's edition, pp. 57–8, vv. 16–19; pp. 59–60, vv. 27–31; pp. 64–6, vv. 56, 57, 59, 54, 50, 55, 53, 49.
11. The *Mu'allaḳa* of Labíd in *Septem Mo'allaḳât*, pp. 90–3, vv. 1–10; and in Lyall's edition, pp. 67–9, vv. 1–10.
12. *Delectus*, pp. 101–2, vv. 11–27.
13. *Die Gedichte des Lebîd*, ed. by A. Huber and C. Brockelmann (Leiden, 1891), p. 6, No. xxxii, vv. 1–3.
14. *Ibid.* p. 2, No. xxiii.
15. *Ibid.* p. 27, No. xli, vv. 1–4.
16. *Ḥamâsa*, pp. 382–5.
17. *Chrestomathie arabe*, by Silvestre de Sacy, 2nd ed. (Paris, 1826–7), vol. II², pp. 134–5, vv. 1–10.
18. *Ḥamâsa*, pp. 242–3; *Delectus*, 30, 8.
19. *Díwán of al-Khansá*, ed. by L. Cheikho (Beyrout, 1895), p. 227; Th. Nöldeke, *Beiträge zur Kenntniss der Poesie der alten Araber* (Hannover, 1864), pp. 181–2.
20. *Díwán of al-Khansá*, ed. by Cheikho, pp. 150–1.

21. *Delectus*, pp. 110–14.
22. *Ibid.* 25, 3. The sixth verse is omitted in the translation.
23. *Ibid.* 9, 11–10, 3, omitting the third verse.
24. A. von Kremer, *Altarabische Gedichte über die Volkssage von Jemen* (Leipzig, 1867), pp. 18–19.
25. *Ḥamása*, p. 430.
26. *Delectus*, 84, 11–86, 2; *Divan de Férazdak*, ed. by R. Boucher (Paris, 1870), pp. 212–213.
27. *Diwan des Abu nowas: die Weinlieder*, ed. by W. Ahlwardt (Greifswald, 1861), p. 40, No. 71.
28. *Ibid.* pp. 28–9, No. 49.
29. *Ibid.* p. 12, No. 16.
30. *Ibid.* p. 27, No. 47.
31. *Ibid.* p. 13, No. 17, vv. 1–4.
32. *Ibid.* pp. 5–6, No. 6.
33. *Ibid.* p. 18, No. 29, vv. 1–3.
34. *Ibid.* p. 39, No. 69, vv. 1–4.
35. *Ibid.* p. 17, No. 26.
36. *Díwán of Abu 'l-'Atáhiya* (Beyrout, 1886), p. 23, 13–p. 24, 15.
37. *Ibid.* p. 274, 5–11.
38. *Delectus*, 92, 16; Ibn Khallikán, *Wafayátu 'l-A'yán*, ed. by F. Wüstenfeld (Göttingen, 1835–37), No. 794.
39. Ibn Hishám, *Síratu 'l-Rasúl*, ed. by F. Wüstenfeld (Göttingen, 1859–60), pp. 151–4.
40. *Ibid.* pp. 440–6; *Elementary Arabic: First Reading-book*, ed. by F. du Pre Thornton and R. A. Nicholson (Cambridge, 1907), pp. 40–48.
41. Extracts from Jáḥiẓ, *Kitábu 'l-Bayán* (Cairo, A.H. 1313), vol. I, pp. 175–88; *Elementary Arabic: Second Reading-book*, ed. by R. A. Nicholson (Cambridge, 1909), pp. 29–44.
42. Extracts from Jáḥiẓ, *Kitábu 'l-Bayán*, vol. II, pp. 86–91; *Elementary Arabic: Second Reading-book*, pp. 46–54.
43. Jáḥiẓ, *Kitábu 'l-Ḥayawán* (Cairo, A.H. 1325), Part IV, pp. 146, 15–147, 13; *Zapiski*, vol. VI, p. 337.
44. Jáḥiẓ, *Kitábu 'l-Ḥayawán*, Part III, pp. 99, 1–100, 6.
45. Ṭabarí, *Annals* (Leiden, 1879–90), I 2247, 1–2250, 13; 2251, 3–2253, 10 (omitting 2252, 5–2253, 2); 2311, 17–2316, 8. R. Brünnow's *Arabische Chrestomathie*, 2nd ed. by A. Fischer (Berlin, 1913), pp. 77–87.
46. Mas'údí, *Murúju 'l-Dhahab*, ed. by Barbier de Meynard and Pavet de Courteille (Paris, 1861–77), vol. VI, pp. 362–4.
47. *Ibid.* vol. VI, pp. 446–78 (extracts).
48. *Ibid.* vol. VII, pp. 204–6.
49. *Ibid.* vol. VII, pp. 38–43.
50. *Ibid.* vol. I, pp. 328–30.
51. *Ibid.* vol. VIII, pp. 19–21.
52. *Ibid.* vol. VIII, pp. 181–2.
53. *Mutanabbii carmina*, ed. Fr. Dieterici (Berlin, 1861), pp. 481–4, vv. 1–22.
54. *Ibid.* p. 182, vv. 3–9.
55. *Ibid.* pp. 532–3, vv. 28–30.
56. *Ibid.* pp. 671–2, vv. 6–10.
57. *Ibid.* pp. 148–9, vv. 2–4.
58. Muḥammad 'Aufí, *Lubábu 'l-Albáb*, ed. by Prof. E. G. Browne (Leiden, 1903–6), vol. II, 8, 17–20.
59. *Ibid.* 10, 13–16.
60. *Ibid.* 12, 11–15.
61. *Ibid.* 34, 20–35, 6.
62. *Ibid.* 35, 24–36, 2.

63. Firdausí, *Sháhnáma*, ed. by Turner Macan (Calcutta, 1829), vol. II, 760, 20–763, 22; 770, 4–771, 8; 790, penult.–795, 23.
64. *Lubábu 'l-Albáb*, vol. II, 29, 12–21.
65. *Ibid.* 43, 11–20.
66. *Asráru 'l-tauḥid fí maḳámáti 'l-Shaikh Abí Sa'íd*, ed. Zhukovski (Petrograd, 1899), pp. 376, 11–378, 14.
67. *Ibid.* pp. 371, 5–372, 14.
68. *Ibid.* pp. 399, 14–400, 6.
69. *Die Rubá'ís des Abû Sa'îd bin Abulkhair*, ed. Ethé, No. 73.
70. *Ibid.* No. 69.
71. *Ibid.* No. 1.
72. *Ibid.* No. 10.
73. *Díwán of Bábá Kúhí of Shíráz*, British Museum MS., Or. 3588, f. 117.
74. Abu 'l-'Alá al-Ma'arrí, *Luzúmu má lá yalzam*, in the Appendix to my *Studies in Islamic Poetry* (Cambridge, 1921), p. 209, No. 2.
75. *Ibid.* p. 210, No. 7.
76. *Ibid.* p. 210, No. 10.
77. *Ibid.* p. 208, No. 1.
78. *Ibid.* p. 225, No. 57.
79. *Ibid.* p. 237, No. 105.
80. *Ibid.* p. 211, No. 12.
81. *Ibid.* p. 212, No. 16, vv. 5–7.
82. *Ibid.* p. 213, No. 19.
83. *Ibid.* p. 229, No. 70.
84. *Ibid.* p. 230, No. 75.
85. *Ibid.* p. 213, No. 20.
86. *Ibid.* p. 242, No. 127.
87. *Ibid.* p. 247, No. 144.
88. *Ibid.* p. 253, No. 176.
89. *Ibid.* p. 258, No. 197, vv. 1–7.
90. *Ibid.* p. 260, No. 198.
91. *Ibid.* p. 285, No. 313.
92. *Ibid.* p. 260, No. 200.
93. *Ibid.* p. 260, No. 201.
94. *Ibid.* p. 264, No. 221.
95. *Ibid.* p. 281, No. 295.
96. *Ibid.* p. 279, No. 286.
97. *Ibid.* p. 280, No. 288.
98. *Ibid.* p. 268, No. 239.
99. *Ibid.* p. 281, No. 296.
100. *Ibid.* p. 283, No. 305.
101. *Ibid.* p. 261, No. 208.
102. *Ibid.* p. 271, No. 249.
103. *Ibid.* p. 283, No. 304, vv. 1–6.
104. *Ibid.* p. 283, No. 303.
105. *Ibid.* p. 285, No. 312.
106. *Ibid.* p. 265, No. 226.
107. *Ibid.* p. 268, No. 237.
108. *Ibid.* p. 265, No. 225.
109. *Ibid.* p. 278, No. 278.
110. *Ibid.* p. 277, No. 273.
111. *Ibid.* p. 238, No. 109.
112. *Les Séances de Hariri*, ed. Reinaud and Derenbourg (Paris 1847), vol. I, 121–30.
113. *Ibid.* vol. I, 130–44.
114. The *Fársnáma* of Ibnu 'l-Balkhí, ed. G. le Strange and R. A. Nicholson, pp. 88, 14–93, 22.
115. *Lubábu 'l-Albáb*, ed. E. G. Browne, vol. II, 70, 14–71, 12.
116. *Ibid.* vol. II, 74, 6–15.
117. *Ibid.* vol. II, 186, 1–20.
118. *Ibid.* vol. II, 127, 18–128, 12.
119. *Ibid.* vol. II, 136, 14–137, 8.
120. Farídu'ddín 'Aṭṭár, *Tadhkiratu 'l-Auliyá*, ed. Nicholson, vol. I, 59–73 (extracts).
121. *Ibid.* vol. I, 114–134 (extracts).
122. *Ibid.* vol. I, 134–179 (extracts).
123. The *Díwán* of Ibnu 'l-Fáriḍ (Marseilles, 1853), pp. 257–262.
124. *Ibid.* pp. 331–336.
125. *Ibid.* pp. 230–235.
126. The *Tá'íya* of Ibnu 'l-Fáriḍ, ed. Hammer-Purgstall (Vienna, 1854), vv. 680–706.

127. Ibnu 'l-'Arabí, *Fuṣúṣu 'l-Ḥikam* (Cairo, A.H. 1321), pp. 8–14.
128. *Ibid.* p. 282.
129. Ibnu 'l-'Arabí, *Tarjumán al-Ashwáq*, ed. Nicholson, p. 19, No. xi, vv. 13–15.
130. Ibnu 'l-'Arabí, *al-Futúḥát al-Makkíya*, cited in Fleischer's *Catalogue of the Oriental manuscripts in the Leipzig University Library*, p. 493.
131. Ibnu 'l-'Arabí, *Fuṣúṣu 'l-Ḥikam*, p. 250.
132. Jalálu'ddín Rúmí, *Selected Poems from the Dīvāni Shamsi Tabrīz*, ed. Nicholson, p. 26, No. vii.
133. *Ibid.* p. 46, No. xii. 134. *Ibid.* p. 124, No. xxxi, vv. 1–6.
135. Jalálu'ddín Rúmí, *Díwáni Shamsi Tabríz* (Lakhnau, A.H. 1302), p. 532, 10–15.
136. Jalálu'ddín Rúmí, *Selected Poems from the Dīvāni Shamsi Tabrīz*, p. 140, No. xxxvi, vv. 1–6.
137. *Ibid.* p. 152, No. xxxviii. 138. *Ibid.* p. 174, No. xliv, vv. 1–7.
139. Jalálu'ddín Rúmí, *Masnaví* (Búláq, A.H. 1268), Book II, p. 92, 15–23.
140. *Ibid.* Book II, p. 107, 8–17. 141. *Ibid.* Book III, p. 149, 6–11.
142. Sa'dí, *Gulistán*, ed. Platts, pp. 2–9 (extracts).
143. Sa'dí, *Búsṭán*, ed. Graf, Book VIII, pp. 388–394, vv. 174–243.
144. Sa'dí, *Ṭaiyibát*, ed. Sir Lucas White King, No. 53.
145. *Ibid.* No. 11. 146. *Ibid.* No. 41, vv. 3–8.
147. *Ibid.* No. 69, vv. 1–7. 148. *Ibid.* No. 131, vv. 1–6.
149. Maḳḳarí, *Nafḥu 'l-Ṭíb*, Leiden ed. vol. II, pp. 780–782; Grangeret de Lagrange, *Anthologie arabe* (Paris, 1828), pp. 141–44.
150–163. Some of these versions of Ḥáfiẓ are pieced together from verses which occur in different odes, while others are free or fairly literal translations of passages in the same ode. No. 150 = *Díwán* (ed. Rosenzweig-Schwannau), vol. I, p. 2. No. 151 = *ibid.* vol. I, p. 168, vv. 2, 3, and 6. No. 152 was suggested by the ode *ibid.* vol. I, p. 576. No. 153 = *ibid.* vol. I, p. 56, vv. 1, 2, 4, 5, and 10. No. 154 = *ibid.* vol. I, p. 240, vv. 1–7. No. 155 = *ibid.* vol. I, p. 198, vv. 1, 4, and 5. No. 157 = *ibid.* vol. I, p. 170, vv. 4, 5. No. 160 = *ibid.* vol. I, p. 222, vv. 1, 3, 6, and 7. No. 162 = *ibid.* vol. I, p. 366, vv. 1, 2, 3, 6, and 7.
164. *Selection from the Prolegomena of Ibn Khaldún*, ed. D. B. Macdonald (Leiden, 1905), pp. 1, 1–4, 8. *Muḳaddama* of Ibn Khaldún (Beyrout, 1900), pp. 9, 11–11, 5.
165. *Muḳaddama*, pp. 37, 4 fr. foot–41, 13 (part omitted).
166. *Ibid.* pp. 127, last line–128, 16.
167. *Ibid.* p. 151, 3–15. 168. *Ibid.* pp. 170, 6–171, 14.
169. Jámí, *Tuḥfatu 'l-Abrár*, cited in Tholuck's *Ssufismus* (Berlin, 1821), pp. 15–20. The translation is abridged.
170. Jámí, *Bahāristán*, ed. Schlechta-Wssehrd, p. 7, 7.
171. *Ibid.* p. 9, 5. 172. *Ibid.* p. 12, 7.
173. *Ibid.* p. 28, 4 fr. foot. 174. *Ibid.* p. 67, 5 fr. foot.
175. *Ibid.* p. 84, 6.

INDEX

The definite article al-, which precedes many Arabic names, has sometimes been omitted both in the text and in the following Index; those names in which it has been retained will be found under their initial letter. Titles of books, and also such Oriental words as are not proper names, are printed in italics.

Andarín, 8
Anṣár, the, 42, 44, 47
Anúsharwán, Chosroes, 125–30. *See* Núshírwán
Anwarı, 132
Arabs, the, influence of religious enthusiasm upon, 182
'Arar, 5
Arbad, brother of Labíd, 14, 15
Ardashír Bábakán, 57, 125
'aríf, 67
Armáth, battle of, 61, 62, 64
Arwál, 7
Arzhang, name of a pit, 88
'aṣabíya, 182
Asad, tribe, 33. *See* Banú Asad
As'ad Kámil, 24
Asceticism, poems on, 34, 36; sayings on, 50–53, 134–37
Ascetics, Mohammedan, described as kings, 36
Asd, tribe, 24
'aṣída, 61
Assyria, 180
Aswad, the Makhzúmite, 44
'Aththar, 22
al-'Atík, place, 61
'Atík, tribe, 48
'Aṭṭár, Farídu'ddín, 133
'Auf, 50
'Auf, son of Ḥárith, 44, 46, 47
Ázádhmard, 58
Azdites, the, 70

Baalbec, 9
Bábá Kúhí of Shíráz, 101
Babylon, 7
Babylonia, 57, 58, 180. *See* 'Irák
badawí, 181
Badr, battle of, 41–47
Baghdád, 29, 32, 37, 56, 77, 102; the siege of, 66–72
Báhila, tribe, 26
Baḥrain, 7
Bahrám, son of Hurmuz, 125
Bairuzán, 59
Bakr, tribe, 1, 2
balbal, 76
Balkh, 134
Banú Asad, 4, 33
Banú Hind, 2
Banú Ṣalúbá, 58
Banú Shaḳíḳa, 4. *See* Taghlib
Banú 'Ubád, 4
Barmecides, the, 65
Baṣra, 47, 51, 67, 69, 70, 115, 134, 135
Basús, the war of, 1, 7
Battle-field, description of a, 97
Báyazíd al-Bisṭámí, 138–41
Bedouins, contempt for the, 29, 33
Bevan, Prof. A. A., 17
Bindawán, 60
Bisṭám, 140
bizál, 32
Bízhan, son of Gív, 83–96, 163
Blunt, W. S., 8
Browne, Prof. E. G., 98, 155, 185
Buddha, 36
Buddhists, the, 53
Bujair, 1
Bukhárá, 131
Bulghár, 151
Bull, the wild, a name for the oryx, 13; described, 7, 13, 14
Burḳa Wáḥif, 13
Bústán, by Sa'dí, 155, 156
Buthaina, 24
Buzurjmihr, 125, 128

Cairo, 142, 176
Camel, the, compared to a castle, 13; to an oryx, 13; described, 20, 21
Camel, battle of the, 51
Caspian Sea, the, 178
Ceylon, 76
Chaldaea, 180
Chigil, 161
Chín (China), 85, 88
China, 131, 151, 161
Chosroes, 105, 125, 127. *See* Anúsharwán
Constantinople, 4
Copts, the, 179, 180
Cordova, 168
Creation of the world, the, 185
Cremation, 108
Cruelty to animals, condemned, 108
Ctesiphon, 126

dabír, 128
Dáḥis, the war of, 10